STRETCHED OUT ON AMETHYSTS

other books by the author

POETRY
Dawn Visions
Burnt Heart/Ode to the War Dead
This Body of Black Light Gone Through the Diamond
The Desert is the Only Way Out
The Chronicles of Akhira
The Blind Beekeeper
Mars & Beyond
Laughing Buddha Weeping Sufi
Salt Prayers
Ramadan Sonnets
Psalms for the Brokenhearted
I Imagine a Lion
Coattails of the Saint
Abdallah Jones and the Disappearing-Dust Caper
Love is a Letter Burning in a High Wind
The Flame of Transformation Turns to Light
Underwater Galaxies
The Music Space
Cooked Oranges
Through Rose Colored Glasses
Like When You Wave at a Train and the Train Hoots Back at You
In the Realm of Neither
The Fire Eater's Lunchbreak
Millennial Prognostications
You Open a Door and it's a Starry Night
Where Death Goes
Shaking the Quicksilver Pool
The Perfect Orchestra
Sparrow on the Prophet's Tomb
A Maddening Disregard for the Passage of Time
Stretched Out on Amethysts

THEATER / THE FLOATING LOTUS MAGIC OPERA COMPANY
The Walls Are Running Blood
Bliss Apocalypse

PROSE
Zen Rock Gardening
The Little Book of Zen
Zen Wisdom

STRETCHED OUT ON AMETHYSTS

poems

January 13 – September 17, 2009

Daniel Abdal-Hayy Moore

The Ecstatic Exchange
2010
Philadelphia

Stretched Out on Amethysts
Copyright © 2010 Daniel Abdal-Hayy Moore
All rights reserved.
Printed in the United States of America

For quotes any longer than those for critical articles and reviews, contact:
The Ecstatic Exchange,
6470 Morris Park Road, Philadelphia, PA 19151-2403
email: abdalhayy@danielmoorepoetry.com

First Edition
ISBN: 978-0-578-04905-2
Published by The Ecstatic Exchange,
6470 Morris Park Road, Philadelphia, PA 19151-2403

Also available from The Ecstatic Exchange:
Knocking from Inside, poems by Tiel Aisha Ansari

Cover collage by the author
Back cover photograph by Malika Moore (in Meknes, Morocco)

DEDICATION

To
Shaykh ibn al-Habib
(and the continuation of the Habibiyya)
Shaykh Bawa Muhaiyuddeen,
all shuyukh of instruction and ma'arifa
and
Baji Tayyaba Khanum
of the unsounded depths

(with a special bow to acupuncturist Dory-Ellen Fish)

---

*The earth is not bereft
of Light*

CONTENTS

About the Title   10
Not a Moment   15
There's No Place He Isn't   17
The Intelligence of the Ruby   19
A Countenance of Care   20
Inklings and Glimpses   22
One Thing or Another   24
The Worm Family   25
Under the Sail   27
Ruby   29
Ambassador to the Clouds   31
The Giant Elephant's Shadow   33
Sump Pump   36
Big Train   39
Simple Pleasures   41
The Void   43
Incandescence   44
Focus   46
Diamond Bigger Than Paradise   47
Nothing is Said Year after Year   50
We Could Say   52
Someday   54
Silvery Glyphs   55
It's All Just so Flamboyantly   58
Getting Into a Bottle   60
The Broken Chair   62
Oh If I Could Just   64
Figures from History   66
Would a Horse   68
As I Crawl into My Grave   70

It's Been Said   72
Growing Old   75
Speckled Hen   76
A Little Man   78
Armies   79
The Dawn Comes Up   81
The Broken Lover   84
King Scopulus of the Sister Isle of Dragoo   96
I Saw a Sock Sailing   103
Where Our Skeletons Go   105
In This World of Losses and Gains   109
A Round Resilient Heart   110
I Can't Go On   113
Words are Music   115
The Indescribable Joys of Composition   117
The Astonishing Thing   119
The Rendezvous   122
If the Light's Locked in a Loud Place   125
All Up and Down   127
The Wine Seller   130
As Many as There Used to Be   135
Saucepans   137
Nothing Interrupts Reality   141
Runaway Train   143
Stewardship   145
Ghostly White Owl   150
The Colossus of Rhodes   152
Rustic Corner   155
Brown Athlete White Athlete   157
God's Hum   160
Crystal Dome   162

I'm the One   164
Hidden from View   166
Rough Death   167
New Grass   170
Acceptable   172
If You'd Asked Me   173
Belief   175
Elaborate Canisters   176
My Bones and My Marrow   178
The Calabash   180
Great Boat   186
Chessboard   189
Contrary Winds   191
Fifteenth Night of Shabaan   193
Death Called Me Up   195
Perfect Happiness   198
I Can Imagine Right Now   200
Graceful Swans   202
A Bell Rings   204
Reason is the Reason We're Here   206
The Surprise of it All   209
I Asked for a Haircut   212
Counting from Zero   215
Everything is Fragile   217
A Hammer Falling Through Space   219
My Love   221
Midnight Ping-Pong Match   222
The Pleasure of Your Company   223
Severed Head on the Gate Post   226
Assigned Seat   230
The Pen Flew out of My Hand   231

Trumpets and Harps   233
I Used to Think   235
In a Dream   237
Little Boat   238

ABOUT THE TITLE

In around 1966 when I was 26, I was in a car accident in Mexico, thrown out of the back (death seat) of a Thunderbird convertible, going around a bend near the volcano town of Colima, at the western elbow of the continent. Funnily enough, I sailed through the air, got punctured on my legs by some protruding thingies (I think they were the chrome studs that held the canvas top when down that must have hit me in flight as the car flipped over), and landed on my back on fairly soft earth by the side of the badly banked road (in the rain), cracking my pelvis and striking my right elbow (the very map of where we were) in such a way that the ball-socket bone got chipped. Great. I had also a strong experience, while aloft, of heading toward a gray mylar-like film in the air, nose first, and the thought that if I went through it I'd be dead. Instead, I fell back onto the ground, blacking out upon immediate impact, but fully conscious and numb a moment or so later. The driver dislocated his shoulder and was in bad shape. The passenger to his right up front was an athlete, and landed on the ground running, so he could tend to us right away. He was an American like us, and didn't know Spanish, but my first words when he came to see if I was hurt were, *"Mi pluma negra, mi pluma negra"* ("my black pen, my black pen"), which he retrieved from the ground and put in my pocket.

We were taken to the local hospital in Colima, where I met young guys who showed me enormous and really ragged knife-fight scars on their chests and legs, of which they heartily boasted, and I figured were their initiation "ribbons" (as in "cut to ribbons")into macho manhood. My punctures were sewn up, my elbow put in a cast, and I was told not to stand up on my legs for over a month and a half, to let my pelvis heal. No cast could be "cast" over it, nothing to be done but wait for natural bonding to take place. Since then I've always put a lift in my left shoe due to a slight skewing when the two halves healed. And my right elbow, every once in a while, "goes off," as I like to say, into excruciating pain. (I later had to be taken to a hospital in Guadalajara, a Catholic ward for the indigent, of which I was one, and they removed a small bone fragment from my elbow the X-ray "expert" in Colima had missed. I woke up briefly after the operation, looked at a lovely bit of "ivory" on my bed stand, and thought it might make a nice necklace, and went back to sleep. When it was gone upon my next surfacing, and I asked the nurse about it, she said "It was your bone, you looked at it and then fell back, so I thought you didn't like it — I threw it out." I was sorry to miss an opportunity to wear something from *inside* me on the outside. I might still be wearing it around my neck to this day...)

Over the years my elbow has "gone off" a few times to unmentionable heights, and I've sought out reputable acupuncturists, thinking they might best be able to treat the problem. My first was Eliot Cowan, an acupuncturist following the famous 5-element theory (of Dr. Worsley of London), who magnificently, over a few month period, made the pain disappear and stay that way for many years. But upon our move to Philadelphia, in 1990, and having grown surprisingly older in that period (nearly 70 at this writing), the sharp elbow pain returned off and on, and I sought out another such practicing 5-element acupuncturist for treatment. Dory-Ellen Fish of upper Germantown Avenue in Philadelphia, fit the bill and has been treating me for a few years now, to great effect. One day I arrived at her clinic and went into the room where the table is, and found she'd bought a new heating mat, as she explained, partly made from crushed amethysts, which heat nicely, and also have apparently strong healing properties. The word amethyst derives from a Greek root meaning: not intoxicated, and I suppose part of its healing properties, even when heated, include the cooling or "de-toxing" of pain-producing energies (it's purple color deriving in Greek myth from Dionysius' wine-colored tears falling on the statue of a beautiful maiden named Amethystos whom he'd been lustfully chasing, and who'd been turned to stone by the protective goddess Artemis in order that she remain chaste).

I stretched out on top of it (the crushed stones are inside ribs of a protective tubing running width-wise and alternating with ribs of cloth) and immediately felt its healing powers... at which point the title came to me, having just completed one book, and being at a transition point between the end of one book of poems and a new one. Worried about it, as I have on some occasions with my quirky titles, I tried to find another title for the collection after composing a number of poems under its aegis, and found I couldn't really change it. There's an exoticism to it, even a preciousness I try to avoid in my work, and one friend upon hearing the title said: "It sounds like it would hurt." So much for polls (though the title page amethyst *does* have a point — enough to wake us into wider consciousness?).

But it's a curious meaning for me also, since in Sufism the "wine" of God's Light, knowledge and gnosis, is that glorious intoxication that leads to liberation and arrival "in Allah," *(fi-llah)*... Yet, also in Sufism, and in particular that of Shaykh Junaid of Baghdad, outward sobriety conceals inward intoxication, rather than the other way around. Even the God-intoxicated, the *majdhoubs* we have seen in the streets and mosques of Morocco and elsewhere, haloed in their own extravagant and particular light, to advance beyond their "madness" must be contained, and every great *'Arif-billah* (Knower of Allah) has traversed godly drunkenness of one duration or another and been surrounded by the envelope of sobriety to be perfected.

Without going into further interpretations (stretched out in death? A sumptuous sultan languorously reclining in sybaritic luxury?) and as always grateful without question for both inspiration and from whence it all and always comes, I have settled on the title as is, in honor of the moment in which it voiced itself, and in devotion to the Source of all from Whom it comes.

...Stately Spanish galleon coming from the Isthmus,
Dipping through the Tropics by the palm-green shores,
With a cargo of diamonds,
Emeralds, amethysts,
Topazes, and cinnamon, and gold moidores...
— *John Masefield*

There is gold, and a multitude of rubies
but the lips of knowledge are a precious jewel
— *Proverbs 20:15*

Whoever has a radiant beginning has a radiant end
— *ibn Ajiba (commentary on the Hikam)*

Let us express our astonishment before we are swallowed up in the yeast of the abyss. I will lift up my hands and say Kosmos
— *Ralph Waldo Emerson (notebooks)*

One poem proves another and the whole
— *Wallace Stevens*

NOT A MOMENT

Not a moment can be squandered
not a moment can be lost

Grab the rope and swing out
over the abyss

"What rope?" you say
when there are

ropes all around us

dangling at our elbows and lying in
coils at our feet

But invisible to our visible eyes

Our eyes must quit the visible
to see them

They swing in frayed joyance
between visible trees

and if grabbing them proves problematic
just leap in their direction

and you'll catch the catch that catches you
the rope that love flings

What am I saying? No

rope no trees no cliffs

No abyss

but *this!*

Our heart's enough to take us
to the goal

Our hearts surround
incalculable bliss

THERE'S NO PLACE HE ISN'T

There's no place that He isn't
in interstices tinier than between

the crossbar and the *"t"* stem of *"tiny"*

But ask me if I think He's
everywhere watching me

in love's evergreen countenance
of stern forbearance

the way an object casts a shadow
when the light's behind it

onto any wall
pure or impure

and I might as well drunk be genuflecting freely
before mud Chukwu at the

village entrance in Nigeria with the
other pagans only in worse state

since they in ignorance are

worshipping Allah
on the *knob* of His door

(though the door itself be holy)

while if I know He's here but
don't abide

I should know but don't know
there's *nowhere to hide*

                                                            1/14

THE INTELLIGENCE OF THE RUBY

The intelligence of the ruby is its redness
Take the ruby away and the redness remains

The lion prowls behind jungle leaves
and its cunning prowl alone is

what makes it king

When snow falls is it the snow or the
overall flakiness of icy whiteness over all

that so enthralls us?

Your heart and my heart in two different places
are one heart aren't they but with

different beats and
two different faces?

                                        1/14

A COUNTENANCE OF CARE

A countenance of care is worth
the blasphemy of perfection

Trees in a jagged row along the
horizon and the

sky on fire a sharp and brilliant
blue

Whenever we want to be someone else
a drop of dark blood

falls into a pail
and some of the world

shivers under its weight

Zebras are just as good as horses
only more decorative and indomitable

Since there's only one perfection
and *Oh!* though we try and try

and without trying would fall
into darkness

our shout of joy is Perfection's ear
hearing itself against

all our shortcomings

as herds of zebras part to show
a lion's countenance

aflame

and small white birds
flying between them

                                                           1/20

INKLINGS AND GLIMPSES

The inklings and glimpses that we get
of the vast extravagant panorama

The one or two trickles we see of the
colossal waterfall in sun's glare

The oncoming rush of Divine Presence we may
feel on our cheeks though unseen

Are like a hem of the skirt flashing in a
dark night only a few

spangles catching the starlight
of a dancer who prefers quick

glances to prolonged acquaintance
as the cosmos whistles past us on its

way to an ever-expanding eternity

whose shreds and tiny hairs catch on our
clothes and whose

dimensions from which we've come
beckon us to where we're going

though one breath in the Beloved's chamber
might draw in a strand of intoxicating perfume

airborne for a split second before
like ourselves

evaporating entirely away

1/23

ONE THING OR ANOTHER

When you're reading one thing
you're not reading another

When you're saying one thing
you're not saying another

When you're doing one thing
you're not doing another

When you're in a state of increase
you're not in a a state of decrease

When clouds are reflected in a window
the window is full of clouds

1/24

THE WORM FAMILY

The worm family is leading a
quite life under the loam

snug in mud
rehearsing since Lucretius their

cosmic rôle
having taken it up when

everyone but vultures and
a few others rejected it as too

gross and unpleasant

But it took the sweet unambitious
worm family with their

slippery silkiness
who slide through mud and

love it more than the miser his
millions or the gaud her gold

God's humble ones who always
come after

Conversant with our essences
converters into the wine of eternity

our poor temporal juices and fattened
fleshy tidbits

Armless and legless in their
patient pursuit of perfection

to uncomplainingly
gather round us

at our selfless last act of generous
invitation to feast

1/28

UNDER THE SAIL

Under the sail set sail from Ceylon
loaded with ambergris alabaster and pearl

headed for the port of Portsmouth
or around the Horn perhaps and up into

intangible waters as this
poem is intangible and barely propelled

on sheer sound for its making
that could also be its undoing

with all the tiny nails of thought undriven
suddenly and extracted in mid-air

So all the elements and the four stalwart
elements themselves fall apart or fall

onto each other in mortal combat the
fire leaping onto the earth as it so often does

earth heaped onto water to make slush
and that mud slung onto fire to

put it out but fire taking big gulps of
air to outweigh by far the

others slunk off now to their
respective corners to lick their

wounds and fight another day or
night of conflagratory rendezvous

The universe at a tilt among its
stars and ratcheting forward somehow

under God's watchful Eye down through
fogs of atoms to our own hearts ablaze or

heaped over with earth or flaring their
nostrils to take in more air

heading out over black waters just as
those boats in the first stanza

settling sail at last through the welter of
sound outward into a kind of

sea of silence with its lulling
up and down rhythms of our

heartbeats again and again both the
gong of life and death's

tom-toms
navigating us

home

RUBY

A ruby lies at the bottom of a pit —
will I throw myself down to get it?

I can glimpse its far off gleam
(or do I think it's all a dream?)

I've heard about the ruby's size
and long considered it a prize

Is it real yearning that I wish to get it
and moment by moment not forget it?

Or because others tout its rare beauty
that I'd throw myself down so absolutely?

How do I know they tell the truth
and not fabricate out of whole cloth?

That I'll expend myself so completely
to the point of annihilation sweetly

envisioned to be stretched out among stars
in God's Holy Radiance beyond what appears

in bodily existence but then more real
than what before I was made to feel

in a lifelong struggle along an axis
whose earnings are accompanied by taxes

we must pay by our unique tangible existence
of breath and body which maintain resistance

to such death since all our centrifugal force
(to which we cling on determined course)

is life that keeps us trodding the safest road
avoiding such pits where rubies reside

Though such pursuit in its extravagance
seems the purpose of this intricately uncoiled dance

in continuous circles from our initial birth
to death that heralds our arrival on earth

leaving the first womb as we'll have to leave
this world's intricately textural weave

for that other one more silvery and jewel-like in fact
arrived at by death's disappearing act

flung down in such a dazzling ruby-filled pit
that only then can we wholeheartedly embrace it

1/29

AMBASSADOR TO THE CLOUDS

The Ambassador to the Clouds informed me
that beyond the clouds there exists

another universe exactly like this one
but going in the opposite direction

Lily the lapdog taught me the language of
all dumb creatures and it turns out

they say the same things we do
only about 10% worth repeating

and that includes Shakespeare

*"Sunlight through the goldfish bowl is
only half the story"* says the

chorus of Daylight Sprites Society who
line up unseen around every daily occurrence

and see both sides at once
dark side bright side

*"Mendicants who arrive on their knees get
served quicker"* says Jiminy Cricket and

he should know since he's about their height

"Romantic love doesn't always turn out for the

best but how it wears out the

*heart of its wearer is so worth the
wild ride even if it crashes"*

says a sign posted on the Tunnel of Love
and inside you can hear both the

swoonings and the crackups yet
doves are always flying overhead

*"If you're going to spend so much time
chewing chew on this"* says both

the hard facts of life as well as
radiant wonder that leaves the

chewer shaking with joy

The Ambassador to the Clouds has been here
and he knows his way around

both the heavens and the door
out of here so he's worth watching as he

makes his way through the crowd
slowly evaporating like this poem at last

and vanishing entirely away

THE GIANT ELEPHANT'S SHADOW

The shadow from the giant elephant on the
city as he sways in the afternoon

to and fro giving to everything the
illusion of being in motion

or of being alive that very poignant
impression of aliveness that so

catches in our hearts when we
see it as the Monarch butterfly first

emerges from her cocoon and struggles
free and first flies to her

Lord who is Lord of the Open Air

all of this accompanied by the giant elephant's
soft trumpeting as if in victory after battle

or having just crossed the Alps with
Hannibal the Great or at least

Hannibal the Daring

and of course this is all a
fable blown out of all proportion

though the giant elephant is real

he wandered off from the giant

circus down the road where instead of
cotton candy it's Galaxy-on-a-Stick as

stars and galactic clusters are
brought into being there in a misty and

thunderous darkness inside a mysteriously
dark and misty tent to distant

calliope music galactic flakes falling between those
wheezy notes

And now this can't be real that is until
we see the clowns who are atoms tumble in in

bizarre vehicles and even more bizarre
getup goofy shoes wriggling hairs

some spinning some zooming ahead
forming pyramidal shapes or shapes of

organic beings like those slowly
swaying tube creatures undersea by volcanic vents

*Now we're getting somewhere now here's
something plausible we can hold onto*

The very whimsically gorgeous and unpredictable
routines of the universe and life as

we know it taking place within it or

in fact being the very life of it from
top to bottom

all vivified I tell you by God's great
gray elephant offstage and out of

sight who never stops his plangent
swaying not even for one

nanosecond and thank God for him I say
though of course

he's *not* real

SUMP PUMP

"The sump pump by the barn suddenly turned golden" said the farmer

weeping in astonishment

"and the cows all went to sleep at the same time such

peace came over 'em" he said between sobs

"The waves arched up in a huge arch and deposited Arty

safely on the shore" shouted Arty's father carrying him back to the

car *"and it almost seemed like the waves waited there in suspended*

animation to make sure he was OK" he added turning his head for a

last glance at the sea

"She turned to look at me and I swear at that

moment I could see all the way

back to her childhood in Warsaw"

as the old woman rocked in her
chair surrounded by framed photos of

people now mostly dead in the
back room of the retirement home

And the planet turns golden in great
waves from time to time and

who's to say if it's in the
mind of the beholder which is

all right too or if it's that in fact
the planet has turned golden for

everyone at once knowingly or not
from Zambezi to the North Pole

and some see or feel it and turn
golden themselves and some

go about whatever business they go about
in Flatland

and the golden-eyed

Oh God make us always
among the golden-eyed

among Your other
miraculous transparencies

and Your golden wind
blowing through us

                                        2/6

BIG TRAIN

There's a big train rolling into the station
far bigger than can fit on our

usual tracks

There's a big door for us all to go through
far bigger than even our

conception of "door"

There's a world far bigger even than
this one whose blessedness

outshines the sun and whose

sun is far bigger than is needed as a
lynch pin for any galaxy

Yet the right entrance through this
door is the exact earth underneath our feet

and the salutation that gains us entrance
is in the very earthly chant of our heartbeats

just as this which is so far beyond our
conceptions begins with our very earthly conceptions

knowing the choiring disks of galactic edges
rotate just beyond eyesight and earshot

but well within our bodily pulsations
when God's dimension enters them

that is so far beyond us
but which embraces us

to its warm heart

SIMPLE PLEASURES

"The simple pleasures" he said...
How about ascending to the Throne of Allah

and contemplating His Face of Everything
and Nothing at all as it

cascades in the thimble the dewdrop the
beak of the toucan the eye of the newt?

Simple pleasures
like water under the bridge is twice as

furious as water in a basin on the
moon if there is water on the moon

which would have to be heavy to stay in
place, no?

But if we veer off from that
contemplation for even a moment we get

trampled by rhinoceros and licked by bear
to say nothing of spun by Penelope herself

to be woven into the tapestry of life
Rockababy Rockababy Hardcore Industrial

Glue

Each involvement gets deeper in one or the
other this world or the next the

Throne and the God of the Throne
or the mushroom growing in the

shadow of your three-legged stool
on which the elves of imperfection

love to sit in a state of distraction

Simple pleasures in this world of
all simple pleasures

designed especially both to trap and to
liberate once the tumbler combination is

found which is given to each citizen at
birth

if such has actually happened and you're not
still in the womb

I've got one leg that wants to go
and another that wants to stop

at this rate I'm
going around in circles

Say *hello* as you pass by
and wave!

THE VOID

The void can't be

avoided

There

I've said it!

2/10

INCANDESCENCE

In all the ways of looking at the
world why is it there's always one that's

missing?

We talk a good game we play the
game we're game and so the

game is played and the tumblers come
together and the combinations

click or not but that always missing
element makes its punctual

appearance and eludes us and is
never mentioned as if a

bite has been taken out of everything
and we're always dealing with

rinds and fragments shards and

remnants but never the entire
crystal held between forefinger and

thumb through which all the light in the
universe is concentrated and streams

through to our hearts or the

other way around

Saddle the horses for the ride
the night is short and long

See the deer herds on the
mountainside by moonlit beams absconding

Take the cup and drink it to the dregs
and see the gates whizz past us

as we stream through to the
incandescence of the all of it that

we are

2/10

FOCUS

Is it a widening or a narrowing that
furthers us the fastest?

Expand to where we see the edges of planets
out the sides of our glances

or pull our sides in as in a monk's cell
so that less and less distract us?

Sail the Seven Seas deserts and
drought rainforests and plateaus

or turn the heart's focus more and more down as a
lamp is trimmed to burn smaller but brighter?

Speak less see less hear less let
the heart ignite by our blowing on its embers

or go on a long walk in unknown country
handsignaling the natives for food and water?

Neither and all ways are
right and wrong for us

until the flickering light blind us
to the measureless

radiance of His Face

DIAMOND BIGGER THAN PARADISE

A diamond bigger than paradise
was rolled out and displayed on a

black velvet cloth

Some saw it and swooned some
embraced it with their whole bodies

some tried to fall into it and others
tried to chip pieces from its

gloriously glittering facets to
wear to impress their loved ones

But this was not nor was any part of it
a diamond you could possess

and even visual accounts of it were
suspected of being partial bogus or just

exaggerated from mind to mind

But grandeur took hold of us and
blotted out Paradise

We could see our faces and the
faces of our loved ones in its facets

The way it stuck out into our lives
protruding from its black velvet cloth

The black velvet cloth that seemed to
go infinitely on and on behind it

It sits here even now and mesmerizes the
best of us and obsesses the worst of us

who never tire of trying to fit the
diamond bigger than Paradise

into the bezel on our ring finger or as a
jewel to be worn over our hearts

though this diamond so utterly hard
so adamantly diamond-like

dissolves at a true touch revealing
concealed Paradise in the

reverse of its light and
agleam in the very darkness of its

true nature of coal crushed and
blackness squeezed to diamond

beauty in unearthly
pressures

And it's in dissolution that its
brilliance is turned from light rays into

doorways and the display black cloth into

death itself and Paradise into Paradise
as at the first

before it fell into view
and dazzled our imaginations

with its light

                                                            2/13

NOTHING IS SAID YEAR AFTER YEAR

Nothing is said year after year
though we wait to hear it

except from a few and in unlikely places
(mule-dust raised by

endless plodding hooves and
shouts along the way from their

drivers and red-faced angry cooks
who always accompany such expeditions)

that would truly and definitively
orient us one by one and all at

once to what most pleases both
Him and us except that it seems to be

opposite to what it is we always
do and opposite also to where we

always so blithely are thinking it's the

only place to be while it's the
last place which is where we

usually are
and there's no time like the present to actually

go to where that is and be
bathed in radiance

A bell falling through gelatin

A shout heard in the distance
suddenly being in both the immediate

past and the foreseeable future

A horse of pure light who's
always at our side

A grange and an ephemeral
doorway where the sun shines

No two things exactly alike
and nothing that's unfamiliar

A disaster averted

Heavenly moisture

2/18

WE COULD SAY

We could say that everything is a veil
thrown over the Truth

Ship's keel doorknob horse neigh sleigh or
fireball as well as

diplomatic overtures divorce and lavish
marriage proceedings and we

might as well include slipping out the
birth canal as well as slipping out the

life door and even everything beyond except that
once it's the

truth that will be what in our present
earth state is the shiny or dull surface of matter

looking us right in the face with its
blazing naked glory

But we're somewhat comfortable here
sitting in chairs and chatting

while not far away lava spume and
sulfur smoke might fill the sky

and a serene stillness that precedes and
follows each event pervades the air

Our cat is outside the closed bedroom door
crouched and listening

and I can't know exactly what's on her
mind at 3:10 a.m. as I write this

but sense a shapely dimension of
cat alertness and cat concentration

beholden to cats
while I'm praying to hold onto the

same that's beholden to human us
alertness and concentration

The black star-eyed night outside the
bedroom window also crouched and quiet

looking in

2/21

SOMEDAY

Someday I hope to write a real poem

but meanwhile these little tissue paper boats
set out across an unreal sea

in howling unreal winds

in which all hands in reality perish
including myself

and real moonlight continues without us
casting silver scallops across

unreal breakers

2/22

SILVERY GLYPHS

Silvery glyphs seemed to shimmer
in the dawn's first sliver

but no patriarch nor priest from its
lost language appeared to decipher

We held the shards in our shaky hands
and blew the finest dust off their

characters but no cock crowed the
morning in which people spoke and

wrote those words awakening to a
new day of thought and commerce

No one came up to us on the
way to the sheepfolds to

hail us in its words and ask happily
after us

No one came fiercely up and shouted them in our
faces to leave their holy precincts and

return the clay tablets to their rightful
owners or places

A blind breeze trickled across and we
could see some of the dust

lift from their characters' grooves but though we
strained to hear neither did the

breezes remember these words enough to
tell us what they were

mouthlessly saying to no one over and
over in a rock silence deafeningly solid

nor could the huge truck of time rolling past
drown them out nor awaken them

The man who wrote them gave them to the
man who asked for them

or the man who wrote them slipped them
into the woman's basket as

soon as they hardened and she
wept to read them

or the twenty casks of oil by the
wall were accounted for on them and

loaded onto a ship before noon
and taken across snake and serpent

seas to be delivered as well as
announced by this formal declaration

But now it was up there with the

precise language of birds and sloths or

butterflies and banana leaves hibiscus and
stones read only by passing clouds decipherable

only to God

                  2/24

IT'S ALL JUST SO FLAMBOYANTLY

It's all just so flamboyantly sedate and
neutral sitting there

with or without wheels

And God looks once into the quicksilver reflecting pool
and cypress treetops appear to frame the

image caught there before the
sun passes

shedding rays like leaves in its passage
whole earthly footage in

docudrama high definition full color and
total surround sound passing more

swiftly than it did when it first played
at Adam's table spread under

Paradise trees laden with future
fruits and recriminations

Eve is surprised that so much goes past
in so little time

but in the Garden flakes of time like
spangles drift through the foliage at

constant speed and shifting angles
piling up at the foot of the

tree that must not be approached under
any circumstances however crucial

and some of those circumstances
take place now

People are biting coins to see if they're real
but it's coins that are doing the biting

to see if *we're* real as that
tree starts

speaking in a language we
all understand

every word as clear as rain

2/28

GETTING INTO A BOTTLE

Getting into a bottle may be a lot
easier than getting out

especially up that long neck

Getting thrown into the ocean is
certainly a lot easier than getting

found at high sea or on a
desert island the bottle just

bobbing up onto the beach the
hot sun burning down and you

ready to burst out eager for a
stretch or to maybe

run along the shore your toes
squinching into the sand granules

Though from one perspective
none of this is possible

yet from another it's
already taken place

just as alligators slip along a few inches
under the surface their eyes above on the

constant lookout for a tasty treat
yet able at a moment's notice to

submerge completely their prehistoric even
anti-historic nubbly bulk and

reptilian wiliness intact

3/15

THE BROKEN CHAIR

The broken chair reminisces about its
former elegance

fondly recalling each backside that
sat in it as if each were a king

And for that chair each backside was

The sere and blasted tree once
struck by lightning thinks about each

one of its former leaves how they
bloomed in Spring and fell in Fall

leaving bare branches and twisting
off at the stem to make their perilous

ways airborne groundward

The snowflake melting on your
woolly sleeve recalls its symmetrical

perfection as it fell through miles of sky
each point in the crystal so perfectly

defined each delicate crossbeam and finial that
mirrored God's perfection in its beauty

sinking fast in the woolen nap and becoming

a little smudge of water that was

once a glittering magisterial mandala

And the wind recalls its origin on its
way to its destination of calm

indistinguishable from its

blue surrounding atmosphere just as
high clouds lose their shape at last

and all is endless sky as purely
one in all its expanse as ever it

was unborn in its perfect state though
brought into existence from God's

going back through geometric reduction spiraling
back into itself the way this

shape of thought has marched across this
page with the trick penpoint describing its

trajectory but now makes a long slow
reverse coil through its own definite

particulars to a calm and perfectly
satisfied cessation

3/19

OH IF I COULD JUST

Oh if I could just stop a
word in its tracks right here and

not let it go forward or backward
upward or inward but just keep it

perfectly still even stationary until even the
order of things in this room and

this house and this part of the
world come to a

similar halt for even one second
and the starry heavens above

this word and all the sun's
rays come to it and stop

and this word would increase its
potency a million-fold and be a

mountain of formidable magnetism or
simple impenetrable volume a kind of

linguistic black hole but not in a
completely negative sense rather a

boring through the passage of time and
variability of place or even my

own flagrant cylindrical movement of
mind or spirit though the turning

heart continue its pure revolutions
until in fact it's aligned with the

axis of all the worlds by its
incantatory concentration and by the

halting of all else around it crowned
with a vibrational glory to the

Single Cherisher and Polisher of
heartbeats now rhythmic in the

feverish flux of things
struck dumb that moment

by the resulting
inviolable stillness

3/20

FIGURES FROM HISTORY

Figures from history might march onto the
page at any moment but in

different guise or with an offhand gesture

Marco Polo at a little hand mirror
trimming his mustache while
humming a period pop tune

Amelia Ehrhart coming out of the
powder room on her way to
climb into the cockpit on the day of that
fateful flight

Christopher Columbus arranging his
knee breeches in a drawer on board ship
and the ship lurches and they
fly onto the floor in an undignified heap

Cleopatra (one of my favorites) in the
costume of a galley slave in order to
do that famous thing of mingling with
commoners on market day to learn what they
think of her

She has no makeup on and looks simply
dreadful

And so it goes and so do they and

so do we

walking through history half
awake and wholly absorbed in
various disguises and multiple

offhand gestures barely noticed by
anyone but ourselves

as the great gauzy curtains part and we
stride confidently on stage to our
destinies

in not quite the right costume at any
given moment and not having

totally memorized the script though we can
hear it in our heads and almost

repeat its words word for word into the oddly
anti-historical air

3/23

WOULD A HORSE

Would a horse made of rainbows be able to
drink from water made of H_2O

from a pool lying in the indentation
made from two blesséd mountain peaks

moving closer together over two millennia
due to geologically amorous attraction

so that in that crevice made by the
alignment cheek to cheek of igneous rock

a pure water collects into whose
pellucid reflection the sun casts her

most delectable rays?

Because just such an occurrence is
possible in this most impossible of

worlds where the chance sparks of life burst
being glanced off a kind of mathematically accidental

or at least perfectly coincidental
auto-impregnation of elements somehow

cutting from their mold of
forms successive generations and

regenerations of life as we know it
down to the brass doorknobs that

open the doors we go through to the
pencils we take up in our fingers to

write a proclamation or cross out a
useless one

So that really a rainbow horse just barely
substantial out of thin air could

just as easily dip its beautiful head with that
flowing mane of lustrous hair curling into clouds

and with its eyelashed eyes closed in ecstasy

drink from the mirroring water that
reflects all this back to its

Creator between which we are as
wisps of articulate light attempting in our

small way to disappear altogether
before we disappear piecemeal

4/4

AS I CRAWL INTO MY GRAVE

As I crawl into my grave and
turn out the light I ask

if the horses have been fed and the
cat touched on her pink nose

If all the saucers wiped dry and the
grasses grown to their full height

If the moonlight paints the windowsills white
and the bottomless buckets are emptied of their

emptiness

If doors are still rectangular and
open only on one side

and roofs are still on top and keep out
things falling from the sky

If all lovers are with their beloveds tonight
and if not are the main streets swept and

courtyards filled with a majesty of trees
even as the sound of surf breaking and

breaking interrupts their octagonal silence

As I turn toward the dark

I wonder if this turning ever ends or if it

coincides with the world's turning or
even the tilt and pitch of the entire

cosmos in its hurtling course through the
starry highway though it seems to us a

slow ride each one an entire lifetime long

I turn out the light as outside a
light turns on and shows

hillsides of grazing deer who all
lift their heads at once in the same

direction of profiles to induce
heartbreak

Does water continue to flow as water?
Does movement continue in a direction

in which those purveyed by it feel a
liveliness in their limbs and a future in

mind?

Though the heart be expanse inside expanse
effortlessly expanding beyond the confines of the grave

where baby planets come to birth
in nimbuses of pale fire

4/5

IT'S BEEN SAID

It's been said the stars are dancing
that the universe has no edge

that we're streaming through space and
all the aerial bodies are moving

apart from each other at stupendous
velocities that we can't feel but

can be measured against red shift

That everything originated in explosion
which is still trajecting outward and yet

here we are balancing tea cups on
saucers and standing up without

falling over
and I'm calmly writing this down

There are these boulders
huge as planets

suspended like sheer cliffs over their
own abysses in black space

galaxies in various shades of neon
glimmering in suspension or disintegration

like jewelry casting light from ignited centers
of amethyst or emerald or any other

elegant substance far beyond what our
eyes can imagine or mind conceive

soundless in unboundedness? Bounded in
held orbits broadcasting sonorous harmonics?

Like the internal organs of our bodies
these celestial bodies generally unseen

enclosed in their own majesty

yet their even slight physical apprehension
astonishes us

and nothingness floats among them to know
their gorgeous lit-up pinball pegs

luminous eyes of a crouched tiger
peering out of spatial foliage

the very *itself* of itself intimations of
the angelic in huge circles of self-radiance

unseen in entirety by the human eye
but gazed on nonetheless

and that same gaze seeing through us
from our own source that is the

single-most
Seeing

Source of all

4/9

GROWING OLD

Growing old is

making peace with the

fact that we're

falling apart

                                                                            4/10

SPECKLED HEN

"It's a speckled hen" said the realist
placing her on a pedestal for

all to see

*"It's one of God's continuous choristers
scratching the ground to find*

His bounty" said the supra-realist

*"She's the intermediary between an
egg and an egg"* said the pragmatic

cosmologist

"Here's a feather for you" said the
purveyor of high couture plucking one

and putting it in my hat

The bird all fluffed up and head
withdrawn in its neck feathers

gurgled at all this attention or to
ward off all this attention

*"If she bore down at this moment and
one of the planets rolled out of her…"*

"Oh are you granting this barnyard denizen deity status?" said the realist

"Shhh here comes the farmer with an axe" said the fatalist

"Charles Darwin might say she's about to become an airplane"

said the wiseacre among us

Speckled hen speckled hen where's your mother?

It's time to move on

4/14

A LITTLE MAN

A little man asleep

on a giant earth

sat up in bed

"Aha! I'm not *dead!"*

he said

4/15

ARMIES

The armies of the left and the
armies of the right met on the

head of a pin
and the pin itself was stuck haphazardly

into the cloak of the officer of a
particularly religious faction in the

grizzly process of driving some
infidels or other from a particular

mountain citadel whose entire
acreage covered the size of a

postage stamp which was affixed
slightly off-kilter to an envelope

addressed to the emperor by an
opposition leader challenging him in

person to a duel which the
emperor of course would reject and so

their opposing armies would swarm out in
full regalia and battle it out on the

side of a flaking pastry the armies the size of
ants and this particular pastry part of a

scheme to kill off a wildly popular
opposition leader by means of a gift of it to him by

a country known for the exquisiteness of its
cakes but this cake laced with an

undetectable and slow-acting poison

And so it goes on and on in its
inimitably human way while not completely

unknown in the other primates yet
seems to be exacerbated by the long-term

memory systems of human beings of which
writing even poems like this one is

partly to blame
though you could also say such are the

warring factions in the
atomic structure of all matter by God's

decree and you
wouldn't be too far wrong

except that
sustainable harmony and

balance does seem in all
to be the ultimate goal

4/16

THE DAWN COMES UP

The dawn comes up like a
bluish pewter plate tilted

at the window

Somewhere a king is
restless in his sleep

Somewhere a man and a woman
are reciting fervent prayers

before the barrels of an executioner

A fledgling is plucking up its
courage to take flight for the first time

straining at the edge before falling

The one in love with darkness
turns away from the light

It hasn't been that long since the last
volcanic eruption

Clarities come in sudden chunks of time
and just as suddenly evaporate

leaving a fly in a bottle on the windowsill
a signed paper that changes the

fortunes of a nation

a barn on fire with the
animals inside

No one promised a perfect world each
time though perfect in its imperfections

in the eye of the beholder
cleansed by Niagaras of God's Light

A square-wheeled cart would never ambulate
a round wheeled cart never stop

if it had no brakes

God's left nothing unimagined
in the mind of God

And we keep our ears close to the
ground to hear its tremors

A door opened on one side
may be a door closed on the other

It's all a matter of going through
radiolaria of near infinite

complexity floating in the sea-depths
and the dawn's come up completely now

and the *churk churk* of distant birds
gathering for the day

4/18

THE BROKEN LOVER

1

The broken lover sealed an antelope inside the
envelope and licked the

flap and mailed it

He chose the trembling skittish creature for those
eyes of his like deep black lakes and

ears of high alertness

Of course the four hooves were a problem
for not only were they cumbersome but

more importantly they wanted to
run away over the hills and into the woods

The antelope quivered as he slipped it in
with his letter of love-longing written in

invisible ink on immaterial paper

And put a stamp on it of a
winking eye full of tears for it knew

the destination was far and the beloved

dissatisfied though the broken lover

on his one-wheel bicycle kept his

balance as best he could when the
beloved's winds blew all around him and

nearly knocked him down

2

The lover can't be faulted for the
intensity of his love

*(The wild beasts have all been herded into a
small pen and quieted)*

The lover's heart is no playground though
high fireworks can often be glimpsed

splattering above it

*(The city streets are cleared at night
for the moon to do its solitary dancing)*

The lover left his natal land in the
side of Skullbone Hill

No he's on his own among the day lilies and the
dying fires of other people's sanguine views

of what's about to come over the

next hill

and what to do about all the
world's unwanted children

*(The lover's heart has more than the
usual four chambers in which the*

*dispossessed and the possessed might
live in comfort)*

It's a lot colder and wetter outside than
expected

And moss-fuzz trails from tree to tree in
midair linking parts of the

landscape into a green continuum

against which the lover talks in
secret to the beloved and feels

a sudden warmth rise
from the bottom of his clay toes

to the empyrean of his cloudless
forehead

3

Tossing and turning sleeplessly
the lover comes up for air

and surveys the landscape of
live and dead oaks after winter's scourge

"Sleep is not an option" they sing
in their reaching skeletal gnarliness

against a gray sky

"You're either dead or alive" they sing
though they've just revived out of

dead sleep rather than sleepy death

and most go on to grow leaves again
out the ends of their wooden fingers

The lover's eyes like two owls looking out
through nature's holes in the

bark that is his skin

and yet he knows the beloved is near
in the creaking as the wind moves

through the trees

4

Someone asked him to
describe his beloved

and his eyes went blank
and his mind quivered

The world filled up with
rose colored smoke and rose scent

Ferocious beasts bared their teeth
either in greeting or in menace

The high waters of waterfalls
spelled out barely audible words

All around him were clues and traces
like love letters left drifted on bushes

and laying on grassblades as
softly as dew

But his tongue was as parched as
someone fasting in defiance

though he wasn't defiant

and in his ears there was a buzz
as if someone were sending SOS signals

from the Marquesas Islands
and he was too far away to respond

All the tools of articulation were with him
but he couldn't respond

*"How fair how far how hospitable
where do you see her and*

when does she appear?"

His eyes were blank
and his mind quivered

5

But let the lover be a lover
as we all are underneath

our tortoise carapace

and like both skier and ski slope
he's all smooth sailing

Though the night be wound around a
quite tight spindle

still the lover shines

No radiance unknown to his

ascensions

like a window-washer leaning in
on his ladder

precarious against the glass

But his destination is *other*
all other banished

every other however aromatic
chased utterly from his awareness

and in that strange plenitude of solitude
all the noble airs of our atmosphere

circulate

and the beloved's voice carried on them
in all their variegation

to all our ears
listening single-pointedly with

multiple drums

6

A little acorn rolled along the ground
looking for its squirrel

A serial killer didn't know it but he was
searching for his executioner

An electric cloud was
hunting for another to crash into

to make lightning

The crash victim was looking for her
mother in the visits of all her well-wishers

The lover didn't know it but in every
second of his life on earth in every

event going out into the world or
coming in from the world

in every nightfall and daybreak
each time the door knocked and

each time it didn't

in each face he met whether openly
expressive or as inexpressive as a

brick
he was searching for his beloved

whose presence infuses every absence
and whose absence recalls every

presence of light waning over a marsh
with its bronze rosiness or every

lowing of cattle in the dark when a
sudden black fog settles down over fields

or every lighted house with people
moving around inside as well as

every empty house where all its people have died

The lover as if on the open sea in a
skin boat like the early Irish mystics

saw in every wave and every particle

the beloved's face back at him in as

enigmatic an expression as if it
weren't the beloved after all but just

molecules dancing in their absolute
order in space a highly trained

corps de ballet with occasional
inaccurate steps to highlight the

perfection of the rest

and thankfulness poured from his
heart though he didn't always know it

and the eloquent word-order of
every phrase of his was a

love note even in
ungrammatical terms

and every state he was in as well as
both the highest and nearest

reflected whether he knew it or not
the beloved answering him as

only the beloved understood for sure
but which put an embrace along the

lover's arms and an unmistakable
moon-like light in his eyes

7

The lover takes no bow
nor grinds no grain

nor fights no war
that would wound the

flesh of his beloved

The lover steps into the circle
yet is not of the circle

Breathes the air of the world
yet is not of the world

Blesses but curses not
bends but breaks not

It's all to do with alignment

The lover's aligned with what he
loves

Often indistinguishable though
not indivisible

When the torrent comes
the beloved shields him

When waves crash the
bow he does not take

though the water be the beloved
both battering and the

boat battered

The lover leaves his senses to the
world and flies free

and takes nothing with him
but that

into the beloved

gone

                                        4/19-29

KING SCOPULUS OF THE SISTER ISLE OF DRAGOO

1

One evening
King Scopulus of the sister isle of Dragoo

*(upon which I might add
the one true dragon in captivity was and*

*as far as I know still is to this
day)*

while stretched out on amethysts in his
grand drawing room which was

itself drawn in meticulous detail from the

east corner to all the other corners
from east to west north and south

thus giving him royal room to

stretch out at his
ease and

he was looking a bit drawn as
well which is not surprising since

the pencil he was drawn with also was in
need of sharpening though he

lay in a room done in India Ink and
bright non-washable colors so he

could relax slightly out of focus knowing his
environs in crisp lines and crosshatching would

sustain him in all its vivid linearity

And watching a painted sun sink
below the horizon and suddenly

struck by his mortality and the
threat of ultimate erasure

the king summoned his royal
flamingo both to see the

ultimate question mark displayed in its
one-legged stance and

also to divert him for awhile from such
grim and leaden contemplation of

(to put a finer point on it)
the Inevitable

2

If we draw a line from
where we are to some

vanishing point in the distance somewhere
out of sight

we don't know where or when
and see ourselves along its trajectory past

factory and fracture as well as
fibula and fabulous enclosures and

exposures say on a tropical isle or
down a long corridor of redwoods on a

sultry but coolish summer's day with
oceanic roar to our right and the

deep darkness of ancient forests to our
left along which our line extends

though it may also extend over
water or through air as in

fact it must in some way as it doesn't
end with our demise though we may not

in fact go aloft in clouds and our
line turn from black to a

scintillating silver

Yet such a line does exist for
each of us and has along with it

attendant music as if accompanied by
more lines to make staves celestial

notes might melodiously
dance on

3

King Scopulus because he
didn't now how far he extended

was the apex of astonishment at
every crossroads and every

move in any direction was for him
a crossroads

And time itself took place just
before him in space not just

before him nor after him in time

and was for him another apex
so that he found what Allah brought

before him sparkling new and endlessly
fascinating though this didn't mean

that before a clockworks King Scopulus was
dumbfounded but rather that

peering in at the springs and wheels
he knew something about the beating

heart of the universe and its crucially
orderly workings

and he would then look up wet-eyed at his
wife and children and take joy in their

punctuality of being beautiful and
idiosyncratic and if instead he saw his

vizier when he looked up beaming at
him with some good news or

frowning at some bad
King Scopulus would know immediately and

shrug and say either *"Call out the army"* or
"call back the army" and it would almost

always be apt though in fact the king had no
army to call either hither or thither

and he and the vizier would then
laugh in their peaceable kingdom

whose time and space was so
contracted to the point on which and

in which they found themselves

by God's good grace

as well as
forever thereafter

4

*"If I should die in the night
transported through the seven*

*caverns of sleep under unearthly stars
send out a fleet of ships well-fitted*

*to scour the horizon for lakes of
pure sunlight that*

*descend through dark water to the darkest
deeps beneath*

*If I should turn upside-down in the
night to all that is living*

*fly the tiny triangular flags of praise
along spring's newest branches*

*that new fledglings may dart
between them in their*

happy search for seed

*Turn my face toward the central Temple under whatever
moon whether full or gibbous*

*and let the palace windows stay open in a
high and noisy wind or in the*

*soft surf of room-lit breezes that
barely shiver the curtains*

*And bring the whitest horse to watch over
my slow dissolution*

*And if I wake instead of die do all these
things again and let me hear you*

sing your long sweet songs as the

grass grows"

4/30-5/15

I SAW A SOCK SAILING

I saw a sock sailing in the sky
with no foot in it

A farmhouse where the
animals ran the business

A moustache that became a mouth
that gave a speech that

calmed a raging crowd

And yet nobody disappeared without
saying goodbye

No one fell down without
breaking their fall

The round globe turns in space
and we hardly feel it

Day follows night and
we all take notice

Flame puts itself out when it's
eaten its fill

The ocean's bellies are full of
whales and giant squid

The telescope that sees the distance
becomes the distance

Hallucination is often
its own reward

when it isn't its curse

Does a sock with no foot in it
mean we all have to die?

When a room empties
does it erase everything that

happened in it?

The moonlight that falls on our faces
illumines us

God shines a light on us
when we least expect it

No damage is done
that can't be undone

except the death of a loved one

5/19

WHERE OUR SKELETONS GO

1

Where our skeletons go
is not the Skeleton's Ball

They go deep down in the ground
wrapped in our dissolution

Porcelain artifacts among a
rubble of stones

Things found in the ground like
old bottles or traces of colonial settlements

Bone foundations to our ruined houses

Like ribs of an umbrella
they held us up

but are anonymous after all
suffering a universal sameness

Same grin same empty eye sockets
same shoulder joints and hip wings

Unidentifiable as the Mayor of Kettletown or
that great *cante hondo* singer from Seville

or the monster tyrant or the

virgin choirboy or the Olympic gymnast

When the wrapping's gone
and our souls fly free

like smudged signatures at the
bottom of a document

our skeletons attest but in a
general scribble

both unique and identical
one shape fits all

Lovely treasure within us
hard as rock

2

They do dance deep within us
when we want them to

our bones

silent puppets to our commands
whisked along by our whims

while enveloped by us and our
desires to go here or there

high or low

sweet unresisters

Mute backbones to our
every gesture

stone road to our
percolations and brave

perambulations
forward or back

across the China Sea
a dagger in our teeth

or giving bread in Pakistan
to bomb victims

their own bones showing

Mineral roads
our souls walk on

until The
Meeting takes place

and we must
leave them behind

stubbed out cigarettes

raw stumps in the ground

3

But what must it be to walk around
with our skeletons on the *outside?*

"Clank clank" I should think
and a limited facial expression

A kind of malevolent mask that
might actually be benevolent

or at least getting on with the
business of being just one more insect to

another insect for labor or maybe even
soul-mate love at last

a not inconsiderable consideration after all
in the meticulous scheme of things

with the softer parts of us
inside armored plates and hinges

and the outer shiny parts of us
working efficiently at our divinely

appointed tasks

5/23-27

IN THIS WORLD OF LOSSES AND GAINS

In this world of losses and gains
an old rhinoceros squints across the pampas

In this world of rises and falls
a caged canary sings for whatever reason

In this world of uprisings and downfalls
the Niagara still falls spectacularly

and giant clouds of water vapor
still rise in wordless puffs from its basin

In this world of loves and losses
a battered noseless sphinx still

gazes out across curling sands

In this world of birth and death
sparrows in the morning cypress trees outside

are tuning up
or in an early confab head to head

making wet stars of whistly sound
glimmer in the air

A ROUND RESILIENT HEART

A round resilient heart is what we need
connecting to both the

end and beginning of the universe with its
crows and its scarecrows and its

rows of identical buildings and shattered
glass in slivered patterns and

silences between us as well as
volubility on special occasions

as well as the long interior soul-stretches with their
own sunrises and sunsets in

bronze or teak across desert or
tundra rainforest or redwood grove

and that this round and resilient
heart brave the history of things starting in the

middle and working its way to both ends
both end and beginning though from

the middle perspective it looks to us
as though that's all there is

with its savage tigers eating wild
goats and its sea-clams eating tiny

fish who dart away
and the DNA of a clan is writing on

scrolls of capillaries the gestures and
attitudes that lead to both

births and dirges funerals and
baby showers as the tall tree shadows

loom and cast their healing shade
in whose circles below

dancers begin streaming two and
two in perpetual rotation

in imitation of the stars

Our hearts are the silver spheres that
reflect back flatness

The soft humming to herself of the
slave to endure the thorns of harvest

The stoic throb at sea
as the ship founders

The painful admission of
defeat and the poignant

aftermath of survival

A round and resilient heart like a
bouncing planet that

trembles in its orbit

a heart of day long and night short
and the song of both in an

indescribable knot of golden eternities
whose loops within loops

are the untying of our hold on the
world and its

hold on us
with nowhere else to go

but within its own
circular salvation

6/8

I CAN'T GO ON

"I can't go on" said the tailor to his
needle that was pulling

silk through the garment of the king
and the thread sighed as it felt itself

tugged forward and as it slid through the
needle's eye a thin high voice could be

heard lamenting as if played in the
grooves of a record

that the tailor would soon drop his work and
return to the countryside of his birth

and sit in the moonlight with his
head against the bamboo rushes of his

door above the cloud-clogged valley
and the king's garments would be

sewn by inferior men without the
ancient skills and the garments would

hang crookedly off the king's
shoulders and bunch ever so

slightly at his buttocks and thighs and soon
no one in the kingdom would know

how to hold the needle just so and pull the
thread along just so to make

earthly magnificence shine in a

way that reflects the
magnificence of heaven

6/10

WORDS ARE MUSIC

Words are music to my ears
and sentences are sonatas

Outside the birds are
speaking in whistles

In the silence of the heart
sentences are being formed

To the edges of the earth
this music is playing

People pass phrases to each other
taking their solos

Even giraffes utter sounds
below the threshold of our hearing

If you press your ear to the track
you'll hear a train coming

Acute hearing hears the words God
speaks to Himself through His creation

And we're His eavesdroppers
cupping our ears with the

hands of our hearts

into the blackness
of His Light

6/11

THE INDESCRIBABLE JOYS OF COMPOSITION

The indescribable joys of composition
astride a Galapagos bicycle with a

mind of its own as it cunningly
balances on that fine blade of

water a huge crest makes before
cresting and rushing to

shore that high blade-thin
peak of solid insubstantiality and

the bicycle beneath me made up of
hybrid parts from everywhere and two

wheels of alternate flame and waterfall
and a body of congealed nothingness

all this in a feverish rush to catch those
bell-like words in a compositional

row that will somehow

illuminate both wolf's lair and lamb's
vulnerability both the circus as it

sets up in a huge central tent pulled into the
air majestically while lions roar

and struck next day by roustabouts like a punctured
balloon until flat and the lions

angrily asleep at last

Words that catch both the smell of spring in every
infant's vicinity whatever the season

and the lugubrious lily scent that
accompanies death unlidded and

unasleep however remote from where
true lilies bloom

Words that will somehow
string lights along the main street and

flares along side street alleyways
as the sometimes zigzag compositional

bicycle under me careens back and
forth on its way to either

rust against a wall in a drenching rainstorm
or transform its metals into finer

more celestial stuff like spun
angel hair taking off into the lighter and

even more multidirectional
of God's latitudes

THE ASTONISHING THING

"The astonishing thing" exclaimed the
parrot upon recovering from surgery...

"is that in spite of all the obvious signs"
said way under its breath the

roadside sign deep in the Sahara
that indicates how many hundreds of

kilometers it is to Johannesburg...

"and every kind of mercy" whistled the
sea anemone just basking a

bit in its shell in the slop of slosh
of the surf as it hits the beach then

recedes...

*"that we and by we I mean the overwhelming
majority of us"* said a page of present-day

earth's population statistics that happened to
lay open on its metal cart in the

dark basement library archives of the UN...

*"as clear recipients of that mercy over and
over"* roared the actual falls of

Niagara Falls through veils of thick
mist and moisture at the

bottom among barrel stave and bone bric-a-brac...

*"somehow nevertheless and both willfully and
consciously"* said the psychiatric clinic to

itself and by that I mean the actual walls and
ceilings and floors in the dark

late at night and all the
patients either gone completely

out of their minds or asleep...

*"fail to see what's right before our
eyes and in our hearts"* said in a

unison chorus all sea life below the
surface to each other both

friend and foe shark and minnow for one
delirious second...

*"and that's God's audible and visual imprint and
signature with very breath and heartbeat"*

said quietly and unobtrusively
every breath and heartbeat

throughout eternity without letup
forever and forevermore

amen

6/13

THE RENDEZVOUS

The rendezvous is always in a
gentle wind

No that's not true
when the house blows down and the

three pigs are shivering together
and the wolf is at the door

But the rendezvous by candlelit moon
on a trestle over the deepest gorge

when the revolutionaries have
taken over the capital and there's only this

one way out of town and
time as usual as well is

running out…

There's always a gentle wind on our

cheeks and brow to accompany us that
comes from nowhere in

particular or in a moment of
preternatural calm between two

sphinxes each blandly staring into each

other's faces

that's always in a gentle wind

But what I'm actually trying to
say is that the special meeting the

clinching of the deal the totally naked

exposure at the
meeting with our Lord

that divine aspect particular to our
own particularity

is serenaded by a rustling of air in
our direction

and if it's in an avalanche
some of that fury is a

gentle wind and if it's
at the great showdown with

pistols drawn and it's just
too late and already one participant is

bloodily down before the hammers click
in that candlelit moonlight mentioned a bit

earlier in more halcyon circumstances

then there's also a bit of destiny's breeze

and love's harsh treatment atop the
very point of the godly paradox

the teetering tip of it
circled all round by

love's gentle wind

the gentle wind of impossible mercy and
sparrow choruses in nearby treetops

and the opening of the heavens to
soft xylophone music

and the clattering of those melodious
brass chimes whose wind-blown

irritations provide the most soothing
most up-to-date

most last-minute
music

6/16

IF THE LIGHT'S LOCKED IN A LOUD PLACE

If the light's locked in a loud place
go quieter still

And if it's of feathery touch
consult Chinese etiquette for modesty

And if it's held aloft
stand in a dark doorway until

the room is cleared of smoke

Go south if it's east or
north if it's west

Go where it's not

The fingertips tingle with its
exuberance

Smart spaniels dig up truffles in its
glow

The whole world turned inside-out
becomes light

War-torn villages of ruined houses and
rusted tanks flipped over and reversed

shine with a supernatural radiance

Staggering down the middle of the street
calling for water

a dazzle on the tongue

we can't go without it

the heart's beats
based on it

6/21

ALL UP AND DOWN

All up and down one side of the clock
there suddenly appeared a curious crack

and slithering out as if it were sheen
was time itself the old time machine

The rigid minutes swift seconds harsh hours
that rise then fall like hothouse flowers

The days the way they bloom and die
each day seeming to fly right by

Weeks appearing anew each Monday
but before you know it's arrived at Sunday

Months nice chunks with their distinguishable weathers
seasonal characteristics like feathers

Snowy white for winter those three or four
then poking out greeniness the sun adores

Then full throttle summer maybe three or four also
thick humidity clogging the air flow

with a few months at each end as a transition
readying us for the intenser summer/winter position

And years well they seem like a kind of Paradise
we can languidly inhabit full-length and giant-size

And of course that enigma an entire lifetime
whose beginning we vaguely know but whose end no rhyme

can quite capture exactly until the end of the line
that we hope will be blessed with some divine sunshine

Well out of that crack all this time came pouring
till the clock was empty now no longer roaring

with leonine authority over us and our aging
whitening our hairs and our systems enraging

with inexactitudes after lifetimes of perfected abilities
carefully built up and honed so brilliantly

(we knock things down we can't see in the dark
or judge distances as usual then miss the mark)

Well time itself slipped out of the clock
in a ray of light that turned its shock-

value into music its seconds and eons
suddenly melodious instead of shy peons

dredging and plowing the same old furrows
Now time was no longer its slings and arrows

watery and note-filled harmonies you can sing
on your very own lips with your very own heart-strings

Now timelessness swims like a pod of huge whales

or fleets of ships hoisting their sails

or breezes endlessly blowing sub-tropical
from all directions with no single focal

point in space since space goes out with time
Oh no! Wait! We're getting squeezed! Something sublime

is raggedly tattering and splitting in two
until it seems there's no me and no you

since if time and space disappear we're finished
and everything about life is suddenly diminished

or more properly speaking snuffed out at once
so wind the clock up again and let it pounce

its extended claws and grinning fangs
for without it we'd never feel our rhythmic heart pangs

of just about anything both bad and good
that sets itself before us like delectable food

on the tables of the law of the space-time continuum
both sweet and sour in its sweet delirium!

THE WINE SELLER

The wine seller won't water the wine
He'll only sell it full strength

The trees won't stint on their leaves
but push them out to the

ends of their branches

Why should we creep along the ground
like snakes or moles with our

dull eyes turned inward

The dark is no more a place for lovers
than light is as light is unto itself

There he goes again right outside
the window

"Strong wine! Strong wine!" he sings
to no one in particular and the

streets deserted

Though his song only lands on the
ears of hearts who've grown

ears to hear his call

2

"*Strong wine! Strong wine!*" he calls
and the echoes drink it straight

He turns his face
and it flows between the trees

He turns again and the
birds are all enthralled in its delirium

One more turn and we'll all be
driven mad by its fumes

The very air we breathe!

He goes on down the street
and the stars try to cork its

dark bottles with their
razzle-dazzle

3

His license to sell has
no expiration date

No one knows for sure
where he hails from

And his benign face doesn't
betray his ethnicity

Moonlight is its main shimmer
even in broad daylight

(and he can't be seen in full
sunlight nor does he

completely disappear at night)

You'd never guess from the
accent of his voice

that his province vanished
long ago and he now

the sole survivor

Yet in spite of his age
he never seems fatigued

calling *"Strong wine! Strong wine!"* at
every corner and cross-section

edges and latitudes

past all devising

4

The time has come
and he tells it straight

Take his wine full strength
with all its havoc all its

indignation

and he'll reward you direct
with its hallowed consequences

While those around you
sip its dregs

and try its shadowed temperance

you swallow draughts that would make
pigs fly!

In the colossal

catastrophes of the world
even just hearing him pass with his

call is enough to dislodge us from its
indecisive debris

and our throbbing hearts
harmonize with his tune

One drink full strength
obliterates time!

6/25-26

AS MANY AS THERE USED TO BE

There aren't as many as there used to be
Their numbers seem to be dwindling

There used to be so many of them
There's as many as there always were

You could count them all on one hand
There aren't enough numbers to contain them

As some come along others vanish
Where have they all gone? There used to be

so many!

I think there are exactly the same as before
(It was always impossible to gauge)

If you counted one you had a multitude
It's a slippery number you can never seize it

There are always exactly the number there should be
Only God knows exactly how many

They're the stabilizing influence of the cosmos
There can't be a decrease or we'd all disappear

If you've seen one you've seen them all
One alone contains a multitude of multitudes

As we speak their numbers are actually increasing
As one dies their number is refilled

Their numbers can't change it's the one true constant
there can't be fewer than there always were

There's exactly the same number as there are stars
Their number hasn't changed only we have

God knows the number and the waves of the sea
Dust motes in air and the exact number of fish

How many breaths we're allotted in a lifetime
and the exact number of our days on earth

The constants remain
only the variables vary

One is enough
to contain them all

everything else
adds up to zero

6/30

SAUCEPANS

1

The saucepans are arranged on the
kitchen wall

The emeraldine cat's curled up on the
hearth

The smoke in the air slowly vanishes
Horse hoof clomps are heard in the stall

The smithy sleeps in his iron bed
his wide generous wife at his side

Sheep in a distant meadow
baa through the gloom

Is it night or day
on flat earth or round?

Do clouds scud across?
Are the sheaves full of bats?

Do the hearts of earth's inhabitants
contain the key that unlocks the secrets?

Or do they merely circulate like the
sluggish river Malarkey?

Does the horse in his stall
know more than the rooster in his henhouse?

Is the grass on the hill
also bathed in divine radiance?

Is the valley hollowed in the
palm of the hand of peace?

Does the smithy know
his cottage is sailing away?

Clouds in the shape of soldiers
bunch in the sky

Thunder on a distant mountaintop
begins to be heard

Miles away in his kitchen
Chang stirs his morning noodles

Doves in their bamboo cage
begin to coo

A radio blares some incomprehensible
music

The smithy continues to dream his
river-raft dream

Poplars are holding back

from singing for joy

2

The satchel under the bridge
contained a litter of foxes

Where was their mother?
Why were they left in a satchel?

Trucks passed and the bridge rattled
They leapt and tumbled inside the satchel

as best they could

There was one black fox
among the cubs

They wanted to be found
Someone wanted them to be found

The mother lay in a ditch
miles away

The baby foxes had recoiled
at the crack of the rifle

The angels of foxes
had leapt around the room

The woods were full of mysteries
not all of them benign

The baby foxes squealed
after a while

How did they get in the satchel
and who put it under the bridge?

Trucks passed
and the foxes were still

*"Foxes don't belong in a
satchel"* said the

girl as she opened the satchel

7/5

NOTHING INTERRUPTS REALITY

Nothing interrupts reality

Take the Gorgon clomping over the hill
gnashing yellow teeth between which
goat skulls gleam

Or a drawing room in cluttered Victorian disarray and the
mysterious disappearance deepening even with
clues scattered on the oriental carpets and
ticket stubs to Timbouctou stuck in the face
of the ormolu clock

No thoroughbred horses lurching in their stalls
nor sunlight making its gray way through an
isolation cell's ceiling cracks into the
eyes of the sequestered professor

Neither feast nor famine
drought nor avalanche interrupts reality for even one
eyeblink nanosecond as the nanosecond's
eyelids flutter for even just one millinanosecond long

But each heave of ocean as if its roiling stomach were
trying to expel its fishes once and for all

each black sky alternating with a blindingly
pellucid blue or crimson so red it must be
the end-of-the-world's fantasy harbinger riding into
port to warn us again and again of our

mortality whose coming and going barely causes a
ripple in reality after all and even
cascades of upflaming water-lights at the
end of this world's bridge welcoming our

extravagant souls don't throw one drop against placid
reality's forefront nor any of its incalculable facets
elusively as present as a diamond on ice
or an ebony sliver on black velvet or

the eyegleam that begins it all when an
infant first glances round outside the
womb house into this world's antechamber
with its incessant strange music

Like the face veil behind which God's Face is
always hidden and always revealed

Like a hand in the dark that can still fit a
key into its lock

Like the total unfurling of our own lives from
end to end and back again to their Source

nothing can interrupt reality even so much as a
gnat's breath catching itself

overwhelmed by the
sudden happy beauty of its flight

1/8
(en route to Sidi Shikr Conference in Marrakech Morocco)

RUNAWAY TRAIN

The runaway train wanted so much
to be the rabbit browsing peacefully beside the tracks

It smoked and smoked but it
only blotted out the sky

Somehow the hare knew its intentions and
stood up on its haunches in

rabbity compassion

The hot sun bore down as if to
burn away the haystacks

standing in the fields but it
stopped short and merely

warmed the little lake a few degrees
as it lay in its basin on the hilltop

The train flew down the tracks to its
intense destination

Inside its cars people slept or talked read
novels or newspapers with no idea their

train had such unusual desires
as it zoomed past city after city

each one beloved to God and filled with
incalculable blessings with

some recognized and some ignored

And the rabbit nibbled a bit at the
sweet grass by the iron rails

And as the sun went down
hopped slowly and thoughtfully

home to its hutch in heaven

7/11
(written at a concert by the Ibn 'Arabi ensemble in Marrakech)

STEWARDSHIP

1

*"Stewardship of a boat in heaven
or a plot of land on the ground*

*while the orange and blasting winds
assail them*

*A glass of water tilted and ready to fall
A deer caught in a barbed wire fence*

unable to escape

*Even distant things beyond our
visual sphere in an imagined landscape"*

said the intensely dedicated but
melting philosopher looking out over our

expectant faces

*"shouldn't distract us from our love of
the Doer of all deeds and His*

Supremacy

*as we catch the glass and
free the deer*

and swab the heavenly boat
and tend the earthly garden

for if we're there at the crucial moment
doing as we must in a

momentary world

and face the Divine Face with our
failing one

radiance can't help but spread"

He wasn't finished
but the earth shifted

and the moon
sped through its phases

2

Three bears were sleeping in a cave

One got up to snatch fish leaping
up the falls

Who was doing God's work?
The bear or the fish?

A child caught a butterfly

and tore off its wings

He saw his mistake and will never
do that again

*Was he in harmony with
God's Perfection?*

A king assembled dervishes
to dance at his behest

While they danced in ecstasy
his armies were invading their neighbor

Did he sin against the Divine Reunion?

Night covers part of the earth
while the other part is adazzle

Neither lasts for long
and both are always flowing

How can you hold onto the night
when day is breaking

or keep your day-face fully charged
when night comes on?

My heart breaks when I think of
my friends who are suffering

Does that mean God's daylight is
at the flood?

Or that we must all depart this world
in sorrow?

Does that mean night's merciful blanket
is being pulled across us?

We're not at the helm
and would only smash the

boat if we were

The Prince stormed out of the audience chamber
to the horror of the ministers

Who uttered the triggering word
or let the poisoned thought

enter the air?

Who spoke a truth that
rustled the Prince's satins?

In the morning some were lost
and some were saved

One of the lost ones is spoken of and
studied even today and people

weep at his words

The Prince is forgotten

The darkness took him to her
bosom where he lay like a baby

in her arms

The exiled or executed scholar
sits by God's Throne

bathed in its silvery radiance

and rivers flow
where before there were none

This story has neither beginning nor
end as Rumi so often says

except what begins and ends
with God

                        7/13 (Air France to Philadelphia)

GHOSTLY WHITE OWL

There's a ghostly white owl so white
its bones almost show

who flies along the margins of the night
looking not for forgetful mice or stray

baby voles but for open windows yellowish
rectangles of light in which are framed

very elegantly alert hearts leaning
forward toward something unseen eyes

open or closed books open or not but
space is shaped around them and

endless doors are open down endless corridors
and more in the distance are

opening as the corridor rises through a
silvery turquoise element that may or

may not be the sky
and these folks' hearts elongate to a

distant spot that comes toward them
with a mercy so great only one

portion would alleviate all Africa and
China and one drop alone return the

sick to perfect health

And the owl sees this and is an
angel and tells his vision to the

other owls with similar pursuits and they are
also angels around God's Throne

and the people thus engaged in their
solitude are not alone but at a

festive feast so well attended one's
not sure there are any folk left on earth to

do their allotted labors

And this ghostly owl illumined from within
flies to the face of such a person and

from its small beak to the person's
mouth drops a berry whose sweetness

would describe the best of what's to be
found on the other side of death

Then instead of continuing its flight

disintegrates into light

7/15

THE COLOSSUS OF RHODES

The Colossus of Rhodes and the
snowball on the window ledge

both disappear

The great supernova light years away
and a short in the electric system

both go out with impressive fireworks

The great sea leviathan bigger by half
than a normal school bus

and the glad gnat who hovers in a
sunbeam last for their life spans

then vanish completely away

Having had these examples we can only
draw a single conclusion

that the mountain of matter that so
overawes us and the

oceans of vastness that so separate us

and the space both outer and inner
so lushly populated with planetary

distractions that so hypnotize us

are in fact nothing at all before God's
gracious Gaze

and if our gaze is also gracious
we too may see the pure transparency that is

all things in their coming into being
like soft kittens taking first furry-pawed steps

and then their interim being and then their
final farewell having had their

day and said their piece finally somewhat
slinking or at least sweetly

sliding away

so that that radiant Face of God's both utter
beforeness and uttermost lastness

is our sun and constellations our
space and mountainous thrashing oceans

with their whales and space with its gnats in an
intimate dance together and

the breaths we draw in as well as the
ones we expel

God bless each one of them and
each one of us as well in our

absolute vulnerable insubstantiality
after all

7/18

RUSTIC CORNER

There's a rustic corner where
snails congregate to

pass on their snail news

I'd like to be among their company of an
afternoon in a moist shadow with my

shell above me commenting on the
occasional ant or spider passing on its

rush-rush way always in a hurry somewhere of
no importance whatsoever let me

tell you I've been just about
everywhere and it's all pretty much

the same
up wall up garbage can up the Princess's

outdoor garden chair

The view may be a little
different but it's all still

pretty much the same
and then a gardener comes and

throws you in the compost and you're

in heaven

or as close to heaven as I'll ever get
probably closed down by the

time I get there though the
God of snails definitely looks

after us I can testify to that
especially crossing streets

So Mr. Ouspensky
two dimensions are enough for me!

Though I can see how a third
might expand my vistas

and as for all the
others that you mention

I'm happiest on the
underside of a leaf

nibbling away to my
heart's content thank you

satisfied with a

snail's
life

BROWN ATHLETE WHITE ATHLETE

The brown athlete strode up who
outdid the white athlete who

strode up who outdid the
red athlete who strode up who

outdid the yellow athlete who
strode up who outdid the

beige athlete who strode up who
outdid the pink athlete who

strode up who outdid the
blue athlete who strode up who

outdid them all

The crippled pianist sat down and
played Rachmaninoff's Fifth

Piano Concerto flawlessly

The blind archeologist felt down in the
trough and brought up the rare

hominid bone fastidiously

The mute acting coach brought out the
character of Hamlet from the seasoned

Shakespearean actor perfectly

The train stopped on a dime
The airplane landed perfectly

The bus screeched to a halt
The taxi turned around in traffic

Everyone took a bow before their Lord
Everyone bowed with perfect humility

Everyone put their head on the ground
in awe

Everyone lay down to rest at the
same time

Simultaneity is the
order of the day

Unity is the
order of the night

The many become the one
and the one is sovereign

Whoever can't see the horizon
must become the horizon

Don't close your eyes on a
day without delight

Everything turns to dust

And the dust
turns to nothing

                                        7/20

GOD'S HUM

That's God's hum you hear
when everything is silent

When you snap the light out and
lie down in the dark

God's hum from far away and
closely near

Along rose arbors and starlight
in endless sentences of pure sound

in total silence

It moved Noah beyond the barren plain
to see a ship in the mountainside and

build it in the air

It opened canyons to those 1800's
landscape painters to see

golden waterfalls in blue cliffs falling into
green valleys charged with light

The hum that's moved us all beyond our
first crawl to our final steps

as we disappear in the side of an eggshell

hill to the crystal clarity of trumpets and then

to a silence where only God's hum is
heard and it is all form and all

formlessness and radiance on water
and rippling waves of air

more audible than sound itself
love whispering in our ear

7/22

CRYSTAL DOME

In a crystal dome the
size of your thumb

the universe speeds to its
appointed hour amid its

companionable stars in
oceans of a glittering emptiness

that glistens in a puddle of
water on a tabletop in a

draughty hall down from the
main sanctuary where

every noise is amplified and
every silence is in motion going

somewhere where nothing has
ever been before in a

night a moment long as
fleet as a deer's leap across

an abyss of fire whose
turquoise and emerald flames are

cold to the touch and whose
ripples are speech or song alternately

loud or soft and the
sound of shuffling feet the

sound of shuffling feet on wood
in a space no

greater than a blink
nor any longer than its

fluttering duration

Light lit in the last
momentum and then only

God's glance returns to its
first Glancer

and the spark of life to its
first dancer

7/23

I'M THE ONE

The snake that slid alongside the
river shouted *"No! No!* I'm *the river!"*

The reflection of stars in the cistern
pool hummed to itself *"Now* I'm *the stars!"*

The successful surgeon looked at his
knife and thought quite simply 'I'm

the giver of life"

But each must bear what
rocks bear in an avalanche down

to the base of a cliff

And none can say *"I'm the first one down"*
or *"without me the king would*

lose his crown"

There's no room for two
in the space of light

so the wise one abdicates
that only

one full light shine

And the flood of it reach to the
top of the stairs

and the very bottom
where the farthest stars are

7/25

HIDDEN FROM VIEW

Inward character wins out over
outward character the way a

bowling pitch will knock down all the
pins one by one at one strike

Angels will assist you from the
far quarters in unusual harmonies

to keep the innermost machinery running
smoothly and oiled with

exquisite nectars to fulfill your
various vows and intentions

the way a hand reaches out in the
dark for a cup and touches it

and brings the drink to your lips to quench
your most persistent thirst

The heart in its harvest reaps
every grain

Sundown doesn't throw the pall of night
over what's pure

Success comes to the mouse in his
hole hidden from view

7/26

ROUGH DEATH

Rough death rides a battered bicycle
alongside the freight train

asking for the dead to be
thrown out along the tracks

making helter-skelter piles
in the remote hills

No one wants that kind of death

Even the noble cheetah crawls
under brush

Neutral death comes into the doorway
and stands pokerfaced in a

tweed suit and polished shoes
and the triangularly folded pocket

handkerchief has embroidered on it in
sizzling neon pink letters the single word: *Now!*

Here death is slower and doesn't go outside
normal protocol retaining much of its

dignity and not too far off from an
afternoon nap

Antlers in the window at such a death
show a kinship with moose and stags in the

woods whose majesty is maintained on
natural log ramparts below an easy

looping of hawks

Then there's celestial death

This death is barely describable and the one
most longed for by all

Glass walls slide down around this
death through which can be glimpsed

long rolling green hills of
Paradise and valleys of light and

golden sunshine

Something elevates as if pushed up from the
earth and something else rather than

closing in expands outward in all
directions at once to a faint

sound not of the screeching of unoiled
hinges on little mechanical wheels

but the brief assertions of human speech

and the sweet aphorisms of fully conscious people

and lights of all kinds are shed and
slant all around the

celestial death and mercy is

palpable of a delectable taste elusive to
description in any earthly terms

And this is the death designated from long
before the creation for those of a

rank worthy to be so extolled

And as the freight train clatters by
we might hear of such deaths and

conceive of a longing for them
and one never knows if that

longing alone might be
enough to enact it

in the council chamber of the
highest enactments

amen

7/27

NEW GRASS

You can smell the new grass
growing by the wayside

and angels between the grassblades
use a special kind of

butter for their hair

and each plain gray pebble at each grassblade's
base is a precious jewel in disguise

so as not to overawe the
others by its preciousness

The landscape full of secrets in this
light and the light itself in all its

anonymous ubiquity an open
door to another dimension of darkness over

light or light over darkness

in which each of us swims
human consciousness illuminated by its

layer's shedding and unpeeling to an
unspeakable bare core

where all rivers meet and

flow out again

and each angel has its
duty to perform

and each grassblade bends in breezes
to shade it

to perform it

7/29

ACCEPTABLE

Make me acceptable to You *Oh Allah*

Hammer me into shape!

7/30 (69th birthday)

IF YOU'D ASKED ME

If you'd asked me at twenty-five to draw a
picture of myself at sixty-nine I'd have
drawn myself as a wrinkled old wreck
crouched over with a cane and a
weak smile one foot already

firmly in the grave and the
other skeletons in a chorus so
happy to greet me with their
skinny open arms

But now it isn't so on my
69th birthday

Pirate ships are coming in with their
loot and ladies from the exotic East are
ululating at their arrival while
flamingos fly in formation overhead
and beams of light play down on
all of us

feeling no older than I did in my
twenty-fifth year even as some things
function a bit creakier and I'm
happy enough seeing

inner pictures pass by

still malleable and made

mostly of soot

in a transformative burning

The Master Forger

visible only to Himself

Beams of light

in His heavenly forge

7/30

BELIEF

Belief is the coordination of events
with the idea of God

Faith is the recognition of that
coordination with every breath

Illumination is immersion in the
Active Presence of that recognition

and for the idea of God

His

Reality

7/31

ELABORATE CANISTERS

The elaborate canisters by the
side of the road

contained and will contain the rich
nectar enough to

continue the journey though we may not at the
moment know for sure where the

journey will take us or if it will
take us to the goal

These elaborate canisters placed there by
Mercy's hands for our refreshment

kept filled to the brim by our own
enthusiastic intentions for the very

journey itself

whose nectar has been siphoned by
the wisest of bees from the most

fluted of flowers
and soon the idea of a journey itself

becomes lost in the journey itself
and the drink from those canisters

in itself is the environment of our
passage for the journey itself

and its extravagant openings

7/31

MY BONES AND MY MARROW

Some will take my bones
and some my marrow

My vocal chords for flutes
beyond all sorrow

The eye that sees
is not the eye that weeps

Oceans of tears
cannot fill up tomorrow

In a blink I saw it rain at the
end of the world

No rock was left unturned
no river unbloodied

Our bones not ours to keep
nor blush nor whimper

A snake weaves round
the lazy days of summer

A mirror looks blankly back at us
when we're gone

A door that knocks when
no one's there to open

God's not at rest
in some far-off dimension

The taste we taste
is the heart's utmost extension

God's rumor becomes
God's Presence in our stead

The ant that crawls across us
on its way

lives on its urgent errand
another day

8/1

THE CALABASH

1

*"The calabash that broke on the
edge of the universe in the*

*hands of old fox was brought around the
Matterhorn on the last steamboat*

*to be served at the King's luncheon
but alas its pulp splattered on*

*Saturn and Neptune and old
fox brought it up to his lips to*

*chomp when all of a sudden…
all of a sudden…"*— 'The young

orphans each in their individual
beds looked wide-eyed at the

chattery traveler who'd been
telling this yarn and they

began to importune yes importune him to
continue as they stood up in their

muslin nightshirts and began
clapping their hands by the flickering

candlelight at this
point in Victorian London with the

hansom cabs crossing the cobblestone
streets below and young

Hickory Chickling among them the
actual son of House of Lords Minister

Sir Humbolt Chickling the Second' —
"enunciated perfectly the pert

nanny Holly Simmons to the vaguely
interested twins as they were

in their beds for their afternoon
naps aboard the 'Looming Boomer' the

great cargo ship bound for the
new world loaded with spices and

trinkets to trade with the Tlingits or the
Arapahoe whomever they might meet first by the

light of a flicking bonfire on the
shore as they assemble with their

goods displayed before them… displayed
before them…"— drifts off the

old geezer talking to himself under the

freeway overpass the last of the

great storytellers down on his
luck a homeless and ignored

old man in a coat two sizes too
big as

trucks rattle overhead and
above those rattling trucks hover

his guardian angels attentive to his
tales as his eyes grow heavy and his

lips grow still

2

But then a fly flies by
and not just some

inconsequential fly but a
dreamer who thinks to

himself as he whistles past the

old man's nose waking him back
up from the sinking of his tall-tale

reverie

"There's a sad sight even for a
fly as twilight closes its

lantern's hinges and night
comes on in its

usual way" this fly being also
unusually eloquent in his

genetic line from a very Shakespearean
uncle who would often

perform for the young flies freshly
emerged from their pupae stages

for as he'd often say *"all the
world's a stage"* and then

go on to fly around grand
mansions until he'd find an

open window where it would
appear the Prince was having another

fitting for vest and breeches
and buzz around the tea tray to

nibble sugar crumbs and crumbly
biscuit leavings

"Now Edgar" the Prince would chirp

"leave a little room for expansion"

winking naughtily at the tailor who
resembled a fly actually with

two huge popping eyes

until the angels took him to the
cloud regions to cut and

sew for him at last

angel cloaks and
celestial gabardines

3

What's the point of a story like this
when God Who is nowhere is

all around us? The veil

fluttering before us

and multitudes of seekers
before and behind us?

The universe cut in two and
sliced down the middle and still

greater to us than a
dot in a desert

and we only a tiny dot
on that dot

It all God's manifest domain

He the Hidden
as well as Manifest

and we lost in it with our
fingered hands in the air

and the bees of eternity
gathering pollen from their

wavering stamens in the night

8/2-3

GREAT BOAT

We live in the hold of a great boat
moving through the stars

There are no windows in this boat
and it is all window

The rudder's held fast by a
force we can't imagine

The bow's pointed to a
place we'll never know

The high sea and the high air
we breathe are all the same

It is night and navigation is by
celestial lights

There's nothing of earth on this
boat but a few medicinal plants

It may be Noah's Ark with its
genetic doubles

Can you feel it gently rocking?
It's never still

Out the window that is not a window
are the woods the unearthly woods

The deep darkness of the woods
is the deep darkness of the heavens

Our hearts are solar flares
born in the deep darkness

It is not silent here
and the waves are song

A face where the moon should be
looks down and smiles

The whole cosmological realm
is like this smile

The boat is moving in all directions
and goes nowhere

Everyone we will ever love
is on this boat

Where have you heard of this boat before
if not in your heart?

It never lands because
there's never land in sight

God's motions are its motions
and His will its way

Finally we can say

it's all a matter of starlight

Homelessness is its home
and its watery shelter

The Captain never sleeps
in His Divine Absence

If His Presence were any more Present
it would shatter us completely

The window that we look out
is the window that we see

What we see is the
window we look through to see it

It's not ours
but God's alone

Who owns it

8/4

CHESSBOARD

Winter is balled up tight inside
the golden pod of summer

with its green fragrances and
extravagantly exploratory vines

like sleeping sentries to an
ice palace on harsh rocks in

miniature waiting to explode into
advantageous reality when the

time is ripe

And summer is all but forgotten in
the death of wintry woods

gangly and straggly and
bare to the bone of all foliage

like a straight-backed decrepit
landlord holding on with all

might but refusing to die
with steely gazes and a gash mouth

while behind the cold eyes are the
low sizzlings of summer which like

love will melt the dour exterior
eyes first then the parting lips

as everywhere the opposites
parry and duck and meld

into each other at last

A chess board spread out
under a tree and the

tree spread out under the stars

8/5

CONTRARY WINDS

In the contrary winds of the heart lie
the trade winds to the jewels the

ambergris and silks of the Orient

the road studded with
diamonds and stones that leads

past the plainclothes sentries
to the vision of the ivory tomb

where the rarest roses bloom

The winds blow and miles of
dunes are rearranged the

drawing room thrown into disarray
the furtive nighttime creatures

scattered inside the darkest wood
with their ears and

eyes alerted to the slightest sound

But a rope dangles
as if hanging down from a cloud

of twisted hemp or turquoise encrusted
braided lariat of gold one grasp

pulls forward with a heft of
headwinds enough to

see past islands to the main
continent where lavish greetings are

assembled on the shore each
aspect of the journey meticulously

articulated like lustrous
pearls on a single string

No shine lost in that sunlight
that rare moonlight

filtered through a straw
to bring us the

drunken clarities of love

8/6

FIFTEENTH NIGHT OF SHABAAN

A ball of mercury
slides down an incline into a pool

reflecting all the starry heavens
making a whispery inaudible splash

A planet dislodges from its orbit and
wobbles out of tune with its

moons and asteroids following suit
and for a millennia or two a tiny

corner of the universe is in
disarray shivering in disquietude

unfelt by all earthly beings except perhaps
the poisonous tree frog

In a corner of our world
behind a broken sun-baked adobe wall

an extraordinary baby is born
whose exemplary life will inspire

even the plants to grow more generously
and in more profuse abundance

actually felt by a distant galaxy
that to us is just a number with

no name though the baby's name
indicates an infinite number of Grace

(not the baby Jesus peace be upon him
but a contemporary saintly one

known by only a handful as a
paragon of purity who

lives his entire lifetime for
everyone but himself)

on this night O God Your granting forgiveness
for all mistakes big and small

I've inflicted on myself and others
now and forevermore

hoping expectantly for absolution by You and
by everyone whose failings of mine have caused harm

as the mercury sphere descends into its
shimmering original element

and distant-most stars audibly
twinkle in this nearest-most cardiac

element of light

8/7

DEATH CALLED ME UP

In Memoriam Robin Blaser

Death called me up the other day
I almost didn't recognize the voice

Wanted to talk about
butterflies and little white moths

I wondered if it was the old flame game
(jump in and sizzle in the wisdom)

Mentioning spiders and their webs got me
nowhere

Death wanted to speak of more
transcendent things

the far arctic and its blue horizons and
blinding whitenesses and low sky

But death egged me on to go further
and we were right by my side again

as well as reflections in a pool of acid
a pond of silver backing to which

this world is just a mirror and our
movements in it vague irregularities in its

smooth endlessness

I wondered if what we end up with is
absorption in that smooth endlessness no more

rough spots no more jagged edges or
collisions or abrupt stops

The voice went on describing almost
subatomic things no microscope can

see and no heart on this side of things
can witness

and I thought of the antlers of a stag
through which you see fragments of the

forest and until it bounds away in
animal fear and joy your

perspective of the whole is
limited to the spaces between antler shapes

Then the flame concept was reintroduced
that to purity you go through burning

and through burning to wholeness and
through wholeness to nothingness

and then the great blaze of light
holds you more than you've ever been

held before above all
arctics and their radiant splendors

little white moths and butterflies
consumed in their own enthusiasm

brought to bear in the
barest of necessities

This room with its circular window
and a phone call from

death that was nothing but a
phone call from myself all along

8/9

PERFECT HAPPINESS

A perfect bed is made by
perfect hands

The roadway is planted with
perfect rose trees

A perfect piece is played on
piano

Why won't you be happy?

The goldfish seems happy swimming
round and round

or is he?

The horse with a donkey friend
seems happy enough on a

perfect day eating perfect grass

There's a perfect smell of baked
berries in a cobbler

blueberries and peaches and
warm with vanilla ice cream

basically the end of the world

There's a perfect storm brewing
out at sea

There's a perfect holiday at a
perfect getaway but no one's going

Our love is perfect in its
closeness and its leeway

Doesn't complete happiness
follow suit?

                                                            8/10

I CAN IMAGINE RIGHT NOW

I can imagine right now
God's nearness to us

in our blood-throb heart-throbbing pulse of
air waves that never cease

snow geese flying over
distant valleys in a gray sky

and the music it might engender
of a spread chord so vast serene peaks and

convulsive oceans are
wrapped in it in perfect harmony

And I can also right now imagine
our nearness to God in a

humble street sweeper so always
overcome with love for everything he's

mute most of the time with
tears on his cheeks always

aware of God's Presence and in our
most secret moments knowing an

intimacy that tastes of fresh
buttered toast and a dulcet honey spread

so golden it disappears mingled in sweet
golden sunlight or an

exquisiteness so simple so commonplace
we notice even a gnat's joyous

dance of life in bathroom shower or
flittering barn shadows

and of both His nearness and our nearness
made one we might be

mindful and achieve of them in an
instant stretched to eternity where

He dwells and where He
invites us to Him

at the very instant He dwells in and

invites us to Him

8/11

GRACEFUL SWANS

Graceful swans become lumps of coal
floating in a cistern

(though under high pressure they might
turn to diamond)

Flame-red flowers turn to
flames crackling on a hillside

(devastation working its way through
dry salvages)

The saint turns back to a drop
and the drop falls into the ocean

that heaves and churns the drop into its
greater self indistinguishable from all the

other drops of which the ocean is
drop by drop constructed

though at any moment the ocean could
also be turned into a drop and that

drop siphoned back into primordial
moisture in whose choir of earliest

sound the saint would be heard
singing the song of the transformation of

flame into flower and diamond into
swan paddling serenely on a

lake in late daylight under a
looming mountain silhouetted by the

moon

and that mountain and that moon
turned into the spotlight of God's

Presence in which
nothing of Him is absent

including absence
and nothing of anything

other than Him

is present

There's only

Presence

8/13

A BELL RINGS

A bell rings and
peanuts fall into a cup

A rhinoceros eats roses under
a porch but still the

world is a large place where all this and
none of it can happen

unless a bridge stretches and throws
everyone off or a cave closes up with

everyone inside then yawns and
forces them out again

Still one little mirror set on a mountain peak might
watch all passing clouds with

pure passivity and no

clown face disturb its mercury-backed
meditation

Cloud after cloud as if a cappuccino bar were
overflowing with

nowhere in particular to go except
splendidly

exactly
where it's going

8/14

REASON IS THE REASON WE'RE HERE

Reason is the reason we're here
but the heart inflamed by a single note

that's another story!

You can bring all your old grandfather clocks
to the central square to be analyzed and

taken apart spring by coil by hinge by hand
but you won't find why its

sonorous bongs each hour gave us
such satisfaction

*"Take apart yourselves and see what you
find"* I shout at them from a

safe rooftop on a balmy day

The beaches are full of children and waves
some louder than others

Everything is overtaking everything else
soon all the children will grow up and die

and the waves will continue beating the shore and
sliding back beating and sliding back

Ah the stillness between the coming in and the

going out

even for a second!
It's in that moment so precious so pure

that the single note that impassions the
heart is heard and everything else stops

a copper pot beaten by a coppersmith
a magician just about to flip an elephant

a billionaire just before he hears of his
bankruptcy

a skier just before liftoff in the sky above the
crowd

And into that stillness the heart rushes
overcome by a commotion in the

heavens that is not earthly and not exactly
heavenly but which rattles the

gates and the glass in all the windows

and cows think of flying if for
only a second

and southpaws think of playing
concert piano in Sweden

and the night sky thinks of
turning over its deep black velvets for a

choir of rainbow hues so spectacular
eyes flash and souls cry in unhazardous

release just for one
tiny glimpse that lasts longer than an

angel's sneeze and shorter than a
devil's itch but into whose

vast expanse the history of the world could be
tilted and there'd still be room for the

history of Mars and the other orbs

And this is enough for the heart to
recognize God's everpresent audience with

Himself alone in a place of no wind
and in a stillness without stasis

and a voice lifted in silent song
and lips to open for the first time to utter

a word

8/14

THE SURPRISE OF IT ALL

The surprise of it all
is that we exist at all

on this little mountain
called earth

with what little we know
in spite of what we can

show for it

The cloaks and veils so
heavily fallen down

over what's essential
though all the

mechanical things
run like clockwork

and all the engines
puff and boil

Were an angel to appear
with a scroll of light

would it fill our sight?

Are the cloaks and veils

keeping us from

worse behavior?

A sweet zephyr
flows across the earth

dispensing rare perfume
out of God's own store

filtering down through
earthly things

What do we know
of its origin?

What we smell
intoxicates us

to know more

A certain tree
beyond visual representation

A certain river
beyond powers of description

A certain place
home to us all

A certain wonder

germane to our souls

No one knows of it
better than we do

once the cloaks and veils
we hold on so tight to

drop
and are let go

And we hear
the bird of dawn

serenading its heaven

its broken heart
mended by song

8/15

I ASKED FOR A HAIRCUT

I asked for a haircut
and got life imprisonment

(tying my shoes on earth
and walking around)

I said I'd leave a memoir
so no one would make the same

mistakes but the paper's run out and
time's run out and the

mistakes turn out to be stairways
in a holy direction

since the window is really a
starburst and the room's

darkness only heightens that
blazing rectangle of light

always there in front of us
worth walking toward

I asked for a pocketful of rye
and got a banquet at

every turn

Off in the distance horses gallop
incessantly along a descending horizon

and every once in a while a
star falls directly onto their path

I asked for a piece of your mind
and got human consciousness

like an ocean whose caskets of
treasures bob sometimes

nearer and sometimes
teasingly so

Off in the distance
wind is blowing through cypress trees

Sometimes houses fly through the air

Feet on the ground and
heart in the heavens

we proceed with caution
and throw off all restraint

No wonder the rest of us
think we're confused

But a brilliant sparrow
landing in the window

brings the Throne Room's news
and it's enlightenment all

over again for the
mouse family living in the wall

8/16

COUNTING FROM ZERO

Counting from zero
everything adds up to zero

The Spanish Armada
fearsome sea-fighters

Where are they now?

Zero

Goliath whose every
footfall shook the earth

casts nary a shadow

Zero

We set out from zero
adding and adding

traumas and exigencies
roller blade emotions

into and out of things
that dictate our lives

Do they cast shadows
or make any noise?

Zero

Our marvelous dramas
experiences here and there

likes and dislikes and
long held opinions

Zero

And when we're done
and the zeros are piled up

who do we see
through them all?

What Face that is
not our own?

For it's not that nothing exists
but who owns the resonance

Behind zero a
zero that engulfs us all

in a rotund expulsion
that makes a whole

8/16

EVERYTHING IS FRAGILE

"Everything is fragile" says the
balsa boat zooming across the

rippling lake at the slightest breeze

"Everything is heavy" says the lead weight
overboard at sea and sinking fast to a

kelp bed far below

"Everything is everything" says a twinkly
monk doing his dawn exercises on a

cliff high in those pink and gray pinnacle
Chinese mountains looming into clouds

"Everything is nothing at all" says a
wise cricket at the side of the

road until a cricket predator
comes along and eats it

not ascribing to that particular
cricket philosophy

though it be echoed infinitely throughout
the earths and heavens as a

ricocheting light bounced off

energies and materializations and reaches

God's Throne from His place *outside* of
as well as *inside* of and in *no physical relation at*

all to His creation except that He be
majestically

Lord and King of everything fragile
everything heavy everything

everything as well as everything

nothing at all

8/20

A HAMMER FALLING THROUGH SPACE

A hammer is falling through space
a silver hammer is falling through space

and we see it flash as it passes
certain galactic configurations and we

assume by its speed that it's
accompanied by the sound of whistling

not a human whistling but more like
what a boiling tea kettle might make

or a calliope or slide whistle
and this one-note speedster

seems to be free-falling but also
looking for a target

perhaps not a specific target though
it may be in its alacritous diagonal

seeking something that will
stop its trajectory

though continued free-fall may be
its sublime objective after all

having been flung from somewhere
spun end over end out into an

endless other somewhere and
happily reflecting the sun's light on some

other powerful light-source
This phenomenal little tool or

tuning fork now that I
think of it *yes* it's a silver tuning fork

both singing to itself as it falls
and tuning up everything else in the

universe as well

Deep space in all directions
like a celestial crooner for whom

the entire cosmos is its
listening microphone

8/22
(first day of Ramadan)

MY LOVE

My love entered the back way secretly
and came around the front so quietly

it can't be said there were footfalls
or even the whisper of a tread

yet a sweetness suddenly filled the room
and out the window the sun shone and

birds sang in the trees

May I call you my love?
My love my love does my chest

expand to your dimension?

From outside the window the
light pours in and fills it

The sound of water flowing
and the rumble of stars

My love circled round me and
entered me simultaneously

until there's nothing left of me

8/23

MIDNIGHT PING-PONG MATCH

A midnight ping-pong match
is playing among the stars

Atoms careen through space smacked by
invisible paddles

The shadow of the Player Who plays both
sides leans over our hearts

The tick-tock sound of the ping-pong balls
can be heard in our ears among the

singsong of speech and in the
soft darkness of silken silences

But the shadow in our hearts
peers deep inside our souls

and finds inside the same space
as the outer space it finds in space

8/25

THE PLEASURE OF YOUR COMPANY

The pleasure of your company
is in mountain heights

felt from below

The sea raised up against us all
held back by a thumbnail

A forest of redwoods talking with
lowered voices among each other

in case a wandering deer should
overhear them

The pleasure of your company
is in the excision of self from self

and the wild jackrabbits of unruly
desires hopping off in all directions

No one asked to be brought here
it's true and no one wants to leave

once they're here unless it's a
smooth walk out a window on some

kind of light beam
or rolled by ineffable touches out to

a sea of quiet mist and soft Aeolian music

Almost no one wants the light to be
so bright it actually engulfs us

sweeping us off what feet we have
left in such circumstances

Where the peacocks in the trees are
silenced by the louder roar of the

entire sound of His love played on
all sonic registers

dazzling even the scarecrows below
into a kind of life and turning the

crows themselves into momentary
monks of sweet merriment who

turn incandescent under the pressure of their
inner illumination

Ah dear one this is
all the pleasure of your company here

feet dangling over the
ridges of the deepest canyon

as night slides noiselessly into
day and day slips almost unnoticed

under night's door

to find itself in a room so
crowded with sanctity

every bird cries out your name for the
first and last time before divine

deafness strikes every
ear in the universe with the

lost chord sung by the dazzled wandering
choirs of the stars

                                                                8/26

SEVERED HEAD ON THE GATE POST

The severed head on the gate post
started speaking

*"You can't deny where I'm speaking from
though you walk around*

in your only reality —

*Separated as I am from life and from
myself"* and at this he seemed to smile

*"gives me a quite marvelous perspective
I'd never had when head on neck*

*thought and schemed as king of this world
though I was but a thief who simply thought*

the world belonged to me"

Days of silence followed this outburst
though small boys were given a

few pennies to monitor it and
alert everyone if it should

speak again

*"Ouch! though I feel no pain
Hate! though I feel no emotion"*

it finally said one twilight and the
boy ran though town crying out

"The thief speaks! The thief speaks!"
and the whole town gathered at the

base of the stockade wall where the
head was displayed its eyes tight

shut and its grimace carved on its face

*"It's not long now you'll all be
up here with me*

one way or another"

it finally said almost sneering
and people were about to

pelt it with stones to shut it up forever

when suddenly its eyes blinked open
and it fixed its bloodshot

gaze on the crowd below who
let out a single shriek

*"Don't worry your circumstances will no
doubt be more comfortable than mine*

though I also went about my evil ways

in all innocence merrily delirious

with the simple realities
but I see now where I overlooked

one crucial thing in all my meanderings"

scanning the crowd now and his face
softening into a serious frown

"that everything we do is a single thing
which we see best when we're

severed from it and see best
what was lacking from it"

At this an elder from the crowd below
approached with a raised staff as if

to beat the head back into silence or
at least command it to say its

piece then leave us all in peace at last

and the crowd closed in around him

"What is that thing that's lacking then?"
shouted the elder and everyone

waited for an answer

But the head closed its eyes and
pulled its mouth down tight-lipped as

before and darkness closed around the townspeople
until one by one they drifted off into the

night to their varied solitudes and a
young boy took up his post in vigilance

But it never spoke another word and the
sun bleached its flesh away and only a

grinning skull remained on the gate post
eyeless and anonymous

8/27

ASSIGNED SEAT

The assigned seat we're given
will take us to the end of the line

though the terrain we look down on
changes from Arctic to Tropic in a wink

and we enter mist domains so thick
we can only hear the silent drone

that may be just our own ears throbbing
the heartbeat regularity that tempos our flight

from one zero to another through the
most animated of interims in which

it seems anything but zero rules our days
though a zero nightfall befall us all

after all

9/1

THE PEN FLEW OUT OF MY HAND

The pen flew out of my hand
The love flew out of my heart

and circled the square as the moon shone
and revived the dead letters of

invocation that went without reply
or seemed to by their callers

who couldn't identify the response
through their veils of tears

though the response rose its flood all
around them and nearly

drowned them in the love surfs that
drown us every day in the air's

fruit nectar and rose bloom

It's late and early at the same time
and in the arched windows faces appear that

echo perfection even with a
gap tooth here or broken nose there

Each is a kind of waterfall of lights
especially where eyes are concerned

Each a love that goes out and comes
back in the same gesture under the sun

Each roasted from rawness to make us
more fit for stronger doses

until we've been confounded completely
and can't tell where the tale ends or

begins or whether the plot
thickens or thins as it seems to do

both at the same time and every
clue solved as well as made even

more mysterious
a lock of hair an angle of light

that is the Beloved's signature on
everything at once without

cease or inconstancy
in a tower of such resonant bird song

the dawn blushes with envy
and the trees bend to listen to our

greater and leafier
commotions

9/2

TRUMPETS AND HARPS

The trumpets are out and the harps are
playing

and the gallops of horses
clop on the cobbled roads

Ribbons festoon the trees where spies
hide and robbers burst

and blackbirds gather to discuss the
ticklish situation

as the ocean claps its sodden hands
and the blubbery beach

foams and grits its teeth

Barbarous hordes plaster the night with their
shouts and obscenities

while down the road in a candlelit window
a chamber quartet whistles a happy tune

Everyone takes everything for granted
on balmy summer evenings

but when winter comes trust goes
out the window

circulating the graveyard like an
anxious debt collector

Looking for beauty in the sunrise
is a full time occupation

Turning your back on the ugliness that
surrounds us is a

risky business at best

When far cries reach us
we can barely hold back our tears

When a long exhalation
covers the town sleepers are

awakened in their beds

Horses become silent and twitchy
Their riders have gone home for the winter

In a few minutes the
boat will have left the harbor

and gone out to where lights
dissolve into disks of darkness

and only the sound of sighing
soughs between the trees

9/3

I USED TO THINK

I used to think death was the
end of life

Owl in a treetop tearing apart a
mouse

Now I think it's the owl as well

Air around us as we die is death
Air around us as we

die is life

Death and life in the air intermingle

Stratosphere and undersea where the
vents are and bubbles that we

see

Breath in and out as well as
air we draw from

inside and around us

More a light we walk through from
light to light

for He's never far from us in

either-where

life or death

Allah the only

Living One

9/3

IN A DREAM

In a dream there's a lion in a
kind of compound and I'm

in it as well but I'm somehow
made to believe that if the

lion threatens me all I have to do is
climb the high gate and go down the

other side and I'll be safe which
seems quite easily done

The dream goes on and other things happen
but then the lion seems to be

heading my way with foul intentions so I
climb the gate as fast as I can it's

easy the gate has large rungs and seems
made of silver and I make it to the top when

suddenly I see

the lion kind of fly over the gate and
land on the other side to wait for me

and I wake up

9/3

LITTLE BOAT

1

The little boat edged out from the harbor
It was filled with the saints of the

twelve noble latitudes

The full moon was out
reflected in their faces

and they were singing

*"Oh where has the time gone
but into the Time-Creator's pocket*

*Each breath is a clock-tick
that cascades down a mountainside*

and fills a pool below with bliss"

In the original language it
rhymed and rang and sounded like

xylophones and bells though it was
only their voices

They were transporting a holy child
back to its country

A boy of seven who had flown through the
air and landed among them out of

longing to be in the company of God's lovers
and whose parents also longed for such

exalted companionship

Their oars whispered in the water
Their reflection was upside-down to them

and showed each grizzled and wrinkled
one of them to also be youths of seven

whose hearts were elevated on waterjets
and whose song pushed clouds across

the moonlit sky

2

Now deep in the holds of the
hearts of these saints

under the hatches and sails the
natural latches and locks lay secrets

so sweet and deep they could
hardly be conveyed

It might come in a glance or an
outstretched hand to offer a

glass of water or heel of bread to a
hunger or thirst brought to a

particular threshold where the
facade's windows are thrown

wide open to let in light and air

Or it might be best transmitted in a
particular kind of silence such as the

misty atmosphere in a jungle after the
crack of a rifle or roar of a predator

when a long and deafening stillness
takes over until monkey cry begins the

clattery chatter again

Or it might be in a word carved out of
nearly immaterial stuff in all twelve

dimensions and displayed in a
play of light and shade that

best shows off its secret facets
turned slowly in the saint's silent glance at last

as the little boat sets out
across the rippling

moonlight

3

Snowflakes fall through the moonlight onto
the deck where the saints stand

facing sheets of cold across the
dark tundra *etcetera*

And by *etcetera* I mean that though
their faces are icy and their bodies

chilled their hearts are actually
elsewhere where warmth is but

beyond both heat and cold

and even
beyond

where
warmth is

9/6-9/17

ABOUT THE AUTHOR

Born in 1940 in Oakland, California, Daniel Abdal-Hayy Moore's first book of poems, *Dawn Visions*, was published by Lawrence Ferlinghetti of City Lights Books, San Francisco, in 1964, and the second in 1972, *Burnt Heart/Ode to the War Dead*. He created and directed *The Floating Lotus Magic Opera Company* in Berkeley, California in the late 60s, and presented two major productions, *The Walls Are Running Blood*, and *Bliss Apocalypse*. He became a Sufi Muslim in 1970, performed the Hajj in 1972, and lived and traveled throughout Morocco, Spain, Algeria and Nigeria, landing in California and publishing *The Desert is the Only Way Out*, and *Chronicles of Akhira* in the early 80s (Zilzal Press). Residing in Philadelphia since 1990, in 1996 he published *The Ramadan Sonnets* (Jusoor/City Lights), and in 2002, *The Blind Beekeeper* (Jusoor/Syracuse University Press). He has been the major editor for a number of works, including *The Burdah* of Shaykh Busiri, translated by Shaykh Hamza Yusuf, and the poetry of Palestinian poet, Mahmoud Darwish, translated by Munir Akash. He is also widely published on the worldwide web: *The American Muslim, DeenPort*, and his own website and poetry blog, among others: www.danielmoorepoetry.com, www.ecstaticxchange.wordpress.com. He is also currently poetry editor for *Seasons Journal*, and a new translation by Munir Akash of *State of Siege*, by Mahmoud Darwish, from Syracuse University Press. The Ecstatic Exchange Series is bringing out the extensive body of his works of poetry (a complete list of published works on page 2).

POETIC WORKS by Daniel Abdal-Hayy Moore
Published and Unpublished

Dawn Visions (published by City Lights, 1964)
Burnt Heart/Ode to the War Dead (published by City Lights, 1972)
This Body of Black Light Gone Through the Diamond (printed by Fred Stone, Cambridge, Mass, 1965)
On The Streets at Night Alone (1965?)
All Hail the Surgical Lamp (1967)
States of Amazement (1970)

Abdallah Jones and the Disappearing-Dust Caper (published by The Ecstatic Exchange/Crescent Series, 2006)
'Ala ud-Deen and the Magic Lamp
The Chronicles of Akhira (1981) (published by Zilzal Press with Typoglyphs by Karl Kempton, 1986, Sparrow on the Prophet's Tomb, 3 short books, The Ecstatic Exchange, 2009)
Mouloud (1984) (A Zilzal Press chapbook, 1995, Sparrow on the Prophet's Tomb, 3 short books, The Ecstatic Exchange, 2009)
Man is the Crown of Creation (1984)
The Look of the Lion (1984)
The Desert is the Only Way Out (completed 4/21/84) (Zilzal Press chapbook, 1985)
Atomic Dance (1984) (am here books, 1988)
Outlandish Tales (1984)
Awake as Never Before (12/26/84) (Zilzal Press chapbook, 1993)
Glorious Intervals (1/1/85) (Zilzal Press chapbook, ?)
Long Days on Earth/Book I (1/28 – 8/30/85)
Long Days on Earth/Book II (Hayy Ibn Yaqzan)
Long Days on Earth/Book III (1/22/86)
Long Days on Earth/Book IV (1986)
The Ramadan Sonnets (Long Days on Earth/Book V) (5/9 – 6/11/86) (Published by Jusoor/City Lights Books, 1996, republished as Ramadan Sonnets by The Ecstatic Exchange, 2005)
Long Days on Earth/Book VI (6-8/30/86)
Holograms (9/4/86 – 3/26/87)
History of the World (The Epic of Man's Survival) (4/7 – 6/18/87)

Exploratory Odes (6/25 – 10/18/87)
The Man at the End of the World (11/11 – 12/10/87)
The Perfect Orchestra (3/30 – 7/25/88) (Published by The Ecstatic Exchange, 2009)
Fed from Underground Springs (7/30 – 11/23/88)
Ideas of the Heart (11/27/88 – 5/5/89)
New Poems (scattered poems, out of series, from 3/24 – 8/9/89)
Facing Mecca (5/16 – 11/11/89)
A Maddening Disregard for the Passage of Time (11/17/89 – 5/20/90) (Published by The Ecstatic Exchange, 2009)
The Heart Falls in Love with Visions of Perfection (6/15/90 – 6/2/91)
Like When You Wave at a Train and the Train Hoots Back at You (Farid's Book) (6/11 – 7/26/91) (Published by The Ecstatic Exchange, 2008)
Orpheus Meets Morpheus (8/1/91– 3/14/92)
The Puzzle (3/21/92 – 8/17/93)
The Greater Vehicle (10/17/93 – 4/30/94)
A Hundred Little 3-D Pictures (5/14/94 – 9/11/95)
The Angel Broadcast (9/29 – 12/17/95)
Mecca/Medina Time-Warp (12/19/95 – 1/6/96) (Published as a Zilzal Press chapbook, 1996, Sparrow on the Prophet's Tomb, 3 short books, The Ecstatic Exchange, 2009)
Miracle Songs for the Millennium (1/20 – 10/16/96)
The Blind Beekeeper (11/15/96 – 5/30/97) (Published 2002 by Jusoor/Syracuse University Press)
Chants for the Beauty Feast (6/3 – 10/28/97)
You Open a Door and it's a Starry Night (10/29/97 – 5/23/98) (Published by The Ecstatic Exchange, 2009)
Salt Prayers (5/29 – 10/24/98) (Published by The Ecstatic Exchange, 2005)
Some (10/25/98 – 4/25/99)
Flight to Egypt (5/1 – 5/16/99)
I Imagine a Lion (5/21 – 11/15/99) (Published by The Ecstatic Exchange, 2006)
Millennial Prognostications (11/25/99 – 2/2/2000) (Published by the Ecstatic Exchange, 2009)
Shaking the Quicksilver Pool (2/4 – 10/8/2000) (Published by The Ecstatic Exchange, 2009)
Blood Songs (10/9/2000 – 4/3/2001)
The Music Space (4/10 – 9/16/2001) (Published by The Ecstatic Exchange, 2007)

Where Death Goes (9/20/2001 – 5/1/2002) (Published by The Ecstatic Exchange, 2009)

The Flame of Transformation Turns to Light (99 Ghazals Written in English) (5/14 – 8/21/2002) (Published by The Ecstatic Exchange, 2007)

Through Rose-Colored Glasses (7/22/2002 – 1/15/2003) (Published by The Ecstatic Exchange, 2007)

Psalms for the Broken-Hearted (1/22 – 5/25/2003) (Published by The Ecstatic Exchange, 2006)

Hoopoe's Argument (5/27 – 9/18/03)

Love is a Letter Burning in a High Wind (9/21 – 11/6/2003) (Published by The Ecstatic Exchange, 2006)

Laughing Buddha/Weeping Sufi (11/7/2003 – 1/10/2004) (Published by The Ecstatic Exchange, 2005)

Mars and Beyond (1/20 – 3/29/2004) (Published by The Ecstatic Exchange, 2005)

Underwater Galaxies (4/5 – 7/21/2004) (Published by The Ecstatic Exchange 2007)

Cooked Oranges (7/23/2004 – 1/24/2005 (Published by The Ecstatic Exchange, 2007)

Holiday from the Perfect Crime (1/25 – 6/11/2005)

Stories Too Fiery to Sing Too Watery to Whisper (6/13 – 10/24/2005)

Coattails of the Saint (10/26/2005 – 5/10/2006) (Published by The Ecstatic Exchange, 2006)

In the Realm of Neither (5/14/2006 – 11/12/06) (Published by The Ecstatic Exchange, 2008)

Invention of the Wheel (11/13/06 – 6/10/07)

The Sound of Geese Over the House (6/15 – 11/4/07)

The Fire Eater's Lunchbreak (11/11/07 – 5/19/2008) (Published by The Ecstatic Exchange, 2008)

Sparks Off the Main Strike (5/24/2008 – 1/10/2009)

Stretched Out on Amethysts (1/13 – 9/17/2009) (Published by The Ecstatic Exchange, 2010)

The Throne Perpendicular to All that is Horizontal (9/18/09 - 1/25/10)

In Constant Incandescence (2/10 -)

www.ingramcontent.com/pod-product-compliance
Lightning Source LLC
Chambersburg PA
CBHW032040150426
43194CB00006B/356